"*Buzz* is a must-have resource for indie authors. Packed with a wealth of brainstorming activities and dos and don'ts resources, it helps target your thinking about the process and translate your self-reflection into action for the best marketing practices."

—Russell Ricard, award-nominated author of
The Truth About Goodbye

"When I published my first book, I had zero experience with marketing and had no clue where to start. Thankfully, the amazing publishing team at Wise Ink took me under their wing and walked me through the entire book marketing process, step-by-step. Today, my book is a bestseller and has been read by people all around the world. [. . .] *Buzz* really is the ultimate guide to book marketing, and essential reading for all authors who want to successful in today's marketplace."

—Josie Robinson, author of *The Gratitude Jar:
A Simple Guide to Creating Miracles*

"This book recognizes the importance of speaking to its reader in a way that offers confidence and realism in the steps needed to take to begin the marketing process, right through continued use of marketing for keeping books current and relevant. [. . .] *Buzz* creates a sense of 'you got this' and 'keep going,' matching the anxiety of the new author and the overwhelming nature of known and unknown things to come for the experienced author."

—Kim Kane, award-nominated author of
Sparkle On: Women Aging in Gratitude

"*Buzz* is a fantastic resource for all authors. It doesn' ʳ you're just starting out or if you're a year or two into your journey—you will lea ʳng your book. [. . .] I wish we'd had this book when we st ɔ doubt we'll be making good use of it now."

—Kathy Engen and Linda Heath, founders oɪ ɔ▪▪▪. park and authors of *GoL: A Curated Guide to the Modern Day Job Hunt*

BUZZ

THE ULTIMATE GUIDE
BOOK MARKETING

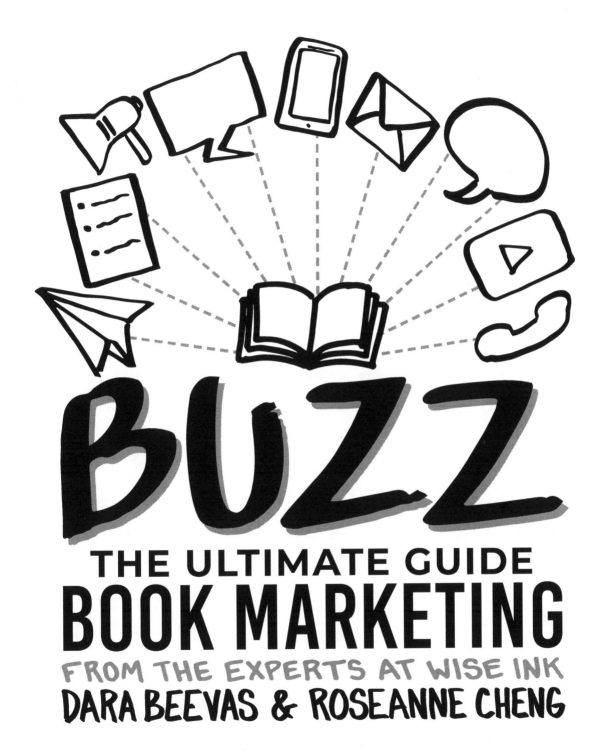

BUZZ

THE ULTIMATE GUIDE
BOOK MARKETING
FROM THE EXPERTS AT WISE INK
DARA BEEVAS & ROSEANNE CHENG

WISE INK PUBLISHING
— MINNEAPOLIS, MN —

Also by Dara Beevas:

The Indie Author Revolution

Also by Roseanne Cheng:

The Take Back of Lincoln Junior High

Edge the Bare Garden

ISBN: 978-1-63489-168-4
Library of Congress Catalog Number: 2018956988
Printed in the United States of America
First Printing: 2018
23 22 21 20 19   5 4 3 2 1

Book design by Athena Currier

Wise Ink Creative Publishing.
807 Broadway St. NE, Suite 46
Minneapolis, MN 55413
wiseink.com

To my family at Wise Ink. You are the hardest-working group of book professionals, authors, and change agents on the planet. You teach me so much.

To Genesis and Tomme. Thank you for making every day incredible.

—Dara

To the writers out there who continue to create, hustle, grow, and make the world a better place with their words.

—Roseanne

Founders of Wise Ink Creative Publishing

From the moment we launched our blog more than five years ago, we've loved dreaming big with authors. Our blog, which began as a hobby, expanded and morphed into Wise Ink Creative Publishing. Today, as we sit with authors, we don't just create tons of checklists (although we use plenty of those) we help them envision the path they want their book to take. We start at the foundation—why they created their books in the first place. We design plans with their big picture in mind, and even after we've crossed big things off our lists (we kinda love lists around here), we urge our authors to go deeper, think grander, and ask the questions most authors don't. We know from experience that authors, like you, go the furthest when they connect their purpose to all facets of their book and beyond.

With book marketing, there is always more—more ideas to execute, more articles to write, more blogs to post, and more events to attend. But the author who does the most isn't always the most successful; the real difference in authors is between those who market with intention and those who don't.

Authors who have clarity make wiser choices. When you know why you wrote your book, the problems it solves, and the readers it serves, you will know what to try, what to risk, and where to spend your time and money.

Our goal in writing this book was to create a tool that might accompany you on the journey ahead—a journey that will at times be fun but will also require moments of pause to regroup, recharge, and reenergize. The trick is to remember the reason writing is important to you—the incredible purpose behind *why* you wrote your book in the first place. Hold tightly to that *why* and use it as your guiding light. Never lose sight of your mission. Millions of people dream of becoming an author. You're the brave soul making your dream a reality. But publishing your book is only the beginning. To engage your readers, make an impact, inspire like-minded ambassadors, and reach your goals, you will need to chart the course ahead. After all, you're about to do big things.

Recently, we sat down to lunch with one of our favorite authors—let's call her Rachel—to discuss her book about practicing gratitude and the accompanying journal. She's done all the right things and has created a platform bigger than her two books. She's a speaker, blogger, and creator of an additional product that she sells alongside her books. She's a master at creating buzz. Now that her books have been published for more than three years, Rachel is pausing. She's planning the next leg of her journey. Between bites, we discussed her plans going forward.

As we ran down our list of questions and collected intel on her most effective marketing strategies, Rachel exhaled and declared, "The smartest thing I did for my books was realize I was selling a book with purpose. The purpose being to uplift and inspire as many people as possible to create positive change in their lives using the simple practice of gratitude— which both books have done beautifully. The next part of the journey is to help my readers take this transformation even further—by creating even more joyful and inspiring content or experiences for them."

Our authors have lots of these kernels of wisdom. Effective book marketing—smart strategies that cut through the noise—should come from a place of knowing that the compelling content within your book is ripe for creating experiences that can lead to sales, future books, and a larger platform to do more of what you enjoy doing.

In these pages, we're going to answer the top fifty questions that we know can shift an author's potential to truly make an impact. Sure, we wrote this book to help you market your book. But we think this book will expand *beyond* marketing. As you read our advice, keep this in mind: Your book requires a special ingredient—one that only you can offer. That ingredient is you. Your story, experiences, ideas, and unique purpose are assets. **You are the magical key that will open all the doors.** As you describe your book, discuss your writing process, and interact with readers—from bookstores to strangers in the street—bring your personality into everything. There is no magic template for selling a million copies of your book. Your book will sell if you believe in it and know your reader intimately. Don't underestimate your ability to motivate your reader to think differently, try something new, or escape more deeply into the world of your writing—this is what *effective* marketing is.

Are you ready? We are. The road ahead is paved with your bold, scary goals and big, audacious dreams. Now that you've brought your words to the masses with intention and confidence, the next step is to start more conversations and keep those conversations going. You've got this.

Remember: Throughout your authorship journey, we're here. Keep in touch with us. Share your questions. And when the going gets tough, dig in, remember your purpose, and keep writing.

facebook.com/WiseInkPub

instagram.com/wise_ink

pinterest.com/wiseink

twitter.com/Wiseink

Author and Marketing Director at Wise Ink Creative Publishing

When I independently published my first book in 2013, I felt the way that many of you reading this book might feel: utterly overwhelmed. There was so much to do, there were so many questions, and I felt like I just couldn't keep up with all the marketing possibilities. Dara and Amy always tell their authors—one of whom was me—that the real work of being an author happens once the book is launched. They are right.

I have learned a lot since publishing my books, so much that I am now the marketing director at Wise Ink. My job is to help authors like you create a customized marketing plan for their books, one that works for them and their lives. With so many options out there, this involves a lot of reflection and soul-searching. There is no one-size-fits-all approach when it comes to marketing your book, and that is a really good thing. This journey is really what you make of it.

Time and again, I hear from authors that they are intimidated by the marketing process. "I'm so overwhelmed that I don't even know what questions to ask!" I empathize with that completely. This is why we chose to format this book in essential questions. We came up with our most-asked questions so you don't have to.

I made plenty of great decisions on my publishing journey (and some not-so-great decisions), many of which are the inspiration behind this book. My hope for anyone reading is that you can learn from my journey and the journeys of the many authors we've worked with; that you can walk away feeling inspired, empowered, and excited to begin the "real" work of being an author.

CONTENTS

Where do I begin?

This certainly is the million-dollar question. The truth is that you "began" when you started writing your book, saw that process through to completion, and decided that what you'd written was worthy of being brought into the world. So congratulations! You have already begun.

Now that you can check "writing your book" off the list, your next task is to define what success means to you. Yes, "selling books" is a good goal *in general*, and yes, it would be nice if Bill Gates recommended your book for his summer reading list. But success as an author is more complicated than simply selling books. For many authors, being successful means leaving a lasting legacy. For others, it means winning awards in the literary world. For authors who have speaking careers, success might mean having something tangible and desirable to sell to their audience. You are guiding this journey; you get to create your goals based on your vision for your life and career.

Doing this work at the beginning will focus your marketing efforts. There are literally thousands of ways to market your book. So begin by asking yourself *why* your book is important, *who* you've written it for, and *how* you expect it to impact your audience. If your book isn't solving a problem or offering something new and different, you'll have a difficult time marketing it.

Next, envision the next three to five years. Are you hoping to start a business? Become a career writer? Launch an online platform based on your book's content? Inspire activists? Is your book the start of several books you will write? If so, who are these future books for? Are you growing a robust online business where content is essential to grow and leverage your brand?

When seeking marketing opportunities, revisit your definition of success and measure whether each potential marketing effort helps meet your specific goals. What works for someone else's book won't always work for yours. If an opportunity does not advance you toward your vision, skip it.

What are three nonmonetary definitions of success that align with your vision for your life, career, and future? Ideas include launching a business, becoming a career writer, or raising awareness for a cause.

My Definition of Success:

1. _____

_____

2. _____

_____

3. _____

_____

With marketing, your work begins from the first moment you tell someone that you are publishing a book. This is the first unconscious marketing you will do, and it's the most essential. Each person in your network has the power to tell a few other people, and they in turn have the power to tell a few *more* people. Merely mentioning your book in passing is marketing. So don't be shy, and don't sell yourself short. Be proud of your accomplishments, and be excited to let the world know that you have something important to share.

If you already have a huge platform or fanbase, congratulations! You have already done marketing legwork and can tap into that base to spread the word about your book. If you don't have a platform yet, your marketing work begins here.

Building an author platform is going to look very different for each individual author. For some, it will mean getting "likes" on your new Facebook page; for others, it will mean expanding your network on LinkedIn. For most authors, it will be a combination of a few different things: building an email list, attending events, taking part in social media, blogging, and contributing posts to like-minded publications. Building a brand and platform takes time, so don't be discouraged if it doesn't happen overnight or even over a year.

Be willing to stand out and claim your place among the remarkable voices already out there. Your readers, right now, are receiving excellent content from other authors on the very topic you're writing about. If you're a novelist, there are books on the market right now that are captivating *your* readers. They don't know you yet. And they need to.

In writing this chapter, we couldn't help but be reminded of one of our favorite TED talks. Seth Godin, author of *Purple Cow* and *Tribes*, presented on "How to Get Your Ideas to Spread." It continues to be one of the most-watched TED talks in history more than fifteen years later. Godin makes the case for pushing your idea beyond "very good." He says:

> The safe thing to do now is to be at the fringes, be remarkable. And being very good is one of the worst things you can possibly do. Very good is boring. Very good is average. It doesn't matter whether you're making a record album, or you're an architect, or you have a tract on sociology. If it's very good, it's not going to work, because no one's going to notice it.

> ## How can you build your platform to be better than "very good" without reinventing the wheel?
>
> _____
>
> _____
>
> _____
>
> _____

Most authors have a website. How can you make your website better than "very good"? Most authors have business cards, social media accounts, and a commitment to doing a few things online to sell as many books as they can. You can do better than this.

For example, if you've written a book about gardening, sure, network at already-established gardening events near you and let the attendees know about your book. But then ask yourself, "What do gardeners need that they don't know they need? What can I offer them that exceeds their expectations?" Can you interview one master gardener a week and post their top three tips to your blog? Can you develop your book on gardening into online courses or classes? Can you create a space for gardeners to meet and support each other? Can you create a list of your favorite gardening books and resources and bundle them into a free gift your readers receive in exchange for email addresses? Getting your book noticed—and getting _you_ noticed—requires creating compelling content and then creating opportunities for people to consume it.

If you mean business, building an author platform will be work that never ends. You will constantly be adding, networking, and expanding. Enjoy the process. Experts aren't made in a day. Your favorite author attracted fans one at a time by captivating one person after another. Tap into the passion that prompted you to write your book and then channel your talents, skills, experiences, failures, and stories into strategies that woo your reader over and over and over again.

Once you have a completed manuscript and a plan to either build or tap into your platform, we suggest thinking about your launch. After many years of seeing authors go right from building their book to selling, we added a "launch" step into our publishing process. This was the missing piece, the necessary phase authors weren't building into the plan.

Think about it—when Apple releases a new product, they don't just place it in stores and then move on to the next thing. They announce the forthcoming product months in advance, send samples to key influencers, engage the media, and publicize the launch date *ad nauseum*. Think about what your launch could look like. We'll talk more about launch in chapter 21—but for now, just know that even in the earliest stages of writing and publishing, how you intend to talk to readers leading up to your launch will offer powerful insights about your book's ability to hook its audience.

So to recap, the first steps to begin your marketing are:

1. Set goals. Define success on your terms. Make your goals nonmonetary in nature.

2. Envision the next three to five years. What is the biggest way in which your book is impacting your life?

3. Create a plan. Outline in detail *why* your book is important, *who* you've written it for, and *how* you expect your book to impact those you've written it for.

4. Spread the word. Start telling people about your book. Try your elevator pitch—share with people the remarkable things your book offers.

5. Push the envelope. Brainstorm how your book's content can spread and get noticed beyond the usual and comfortable marketing efforts of most authors. Think big, different, and beyond the book.

6. Try. Test. Repeat. Keep in mind that some of your marketing efforts won't necessarily translate to direct book sales, and that is okay. Think about it this way: your book is just a small piece of your brand and your identity. Some of your efforts can and should be focused on having people get to know you and why they should care to read what you've written.

What does it *really* mean to "market" my book?

Marketing your book is, simply put, convincing readers to buy it. Of course, to convince them, you have to get their attention. Marketing is how you do that. Whether it's through social media, events, or blogging, any effort to grab your readers' attention is marketing.

There's more, though, and this is extremely important. If you want people to buy your book, you will need to market yourself: the writer, the idea, the brand behind the book.

You are a brand. Yes, you. To *really* market your book, you need to brand yourself.

Being a brand is good; it helps communicate your essence and values to the customer. Think about your favorite brands—places you like to frequent or products you buy. Ask yourself: What is this brand's mission? What is its style? What are its values?

As an author, you are more than the words you've written—you are also part of the experience you've created for your reader. Have you ever read a book because you found the author intriguing, admirable, or likable? Similarly, have you ever been turned off by a book because you found the author abrasive or unsavory?

Building a fanbase is going to involve more than just your finished product. We live in an age where it is simply not enough to have an incredible book—you need to have an exceptional presence to complement it. That presence is part of your brand, and your brand is a major way you are going to sell books. It's also the primary way you will reach your long-term, overarching goals as an author.

We know *brand* is a term that gets tossed around a lot these days. It's an overused buzzword. But we know from experience that the authors who connect their content to a vision, a mission, thoughtful keywords and phrases, and consistent color and design choices that appeal to their audience have an easier time determining the right marketing strategies. Certain marketing tactics will be eliminated purely based on not being in line with your brand.

As an author, you are now a public figure. As a "public figure," you'll find abundant opportunities to draw people into you, your vision, your creative process, and your writing journey. This will undoubtedly market your book better than anything else you do.

If you write under a pseudonym, you might think you have avoided the need to be seen as a public figure. Wrong. You have the exact same marketing work ahead of you. If you're trying to keep your writing a secret for some reason, you have the disadvantage of not being able to tap into your organic base of family and friends, as well as the disadvantage of having to maintain multiple personas online. Do you get the sense we don't love pen names? We don't.

Consider how to factor the following items into your overall brand as an author:

1. **Email address and website domain name:** yourname@gmail.com, yourname@websiteaddress.com, and www.yourname.com are all branding decisions that impact your marketing long-term. Consider whether you'll have more than one book. If so, a domain address that includes your name is a better idea than

www.booktitle.com. Buy your name's domain address. Your email and website addresses will be on marketing materials such as business cards, sell sheets, and media kits and may even be in your actual book. Make a good impression here, and think about your three- to five-year plan.

2. **Website content:** The ultimate branding tool will undoubtedly be your website. Everything from your "About" page to the color scheme to the site map tells your audience who you are. This is why, if you choose to have a website, you need to make it good—don't leave it hanging out there with stale updates and old information. Make your website work for you. Market your speaking topics, add behind-the-scene pictures, build your blog into a primary resource for your audience, and regularly provide other resources that can be accessed.

3. **Author bio:** This content will exist in more places than just the back of your book. Your bio tells your reader a lot about you (more on this on page 83) and is more than a few lines about where you studied and what you do for a living. Use your bio to personalize your expertise. Whether it's playful, friendly, or direct, your bio markets your credibility.

4. **Marketing materials:** Your business cards, postcards, event invitations, and sell sheet are incredible branding tools. They should complement your book but also serve as standalone tools that communicate your style, tone, and personality.

5. **Social media profiles:** Your Twitter header, Instagram feed, and Facebook header are just a few examples of places online you can incorporate graphics and colors to communicate your brand.

3

I hate marketing. How do I make this less of a chore and more fun?

Before we answer this question, we're going to have to get a little philosophical.

Marketing your book is part of the deal. It just is. You can't avoid it. Wanting to publish a book but not wanting to market it is the same as wanting to have a child but not wanting to deal with any dirty diapers or sleep deprivation.

So the way we see it, you have two choices: You can either 1.) make this fun or 2.) complain about how much marketing sucks.

We highly recommend the former.

The problem for many authors is that the word "marketing" is intimidating. It automatically sounds like a to-do list of tiresome actions that aren't going to result in an immediate payoff. Trust us—we've written a couple books before this one, and you're right. Inevitably, marketing comes with a few duds, time spent on the wrong things, and the feeling that you're often not making the impact you want. Marketing has rightfully earned a reputation for wearing out even the most resilient of authors. That's why the number-one way to keep it enjoyable is to incorporate marketing into the things you do every day.

This is the secret to smart marketing: Don't add fifteen more items to your plate. Find opportunities in your life *right now* where marketing your book won't work against you. Instead of picking up your phone and scrolling through your favorite websites, use that time to post a photo of what you're up to at that precise moment. Work a marketing opportunity into a destination you were already planning to visit on a business trip or vacation. If you have a writing breakthrough and want to share your advice with the world, do it!

Another tip: use the content you've already created to help market your book.

To our embarrassment, we've discovered again and again that we've created tons of tools, templates, guides, checklists, and blog posts over the years that we simply haven't leveraged. We're so used to creating that we write content, dispose of it, and create it all over again on the next cycle. Then, when it's time to outline new marketing initiatives, we've found ourselves stumped, overwhelmed, or creating something for the second or even third time.

It occurred to us, after a day in the garage catching up on spring cleaning, that we had a content problem. One of our husbands found a dusty box in the corner that contained fifty copies of a sixty-page workshop booklet we'd created our first year in business. We'd forgotten that in the early days of marketing Wise Ink, we'd tried a few different tactics to get authors in the door, including creating one of our best workshops yet. We really overdid it, and our booklet had not only the slides from the presentation but also handouts, resources, step-by-step guides, checklists, and more. We wanted to impress our attendees, so we went above and beyond. Our workshop attracted about twenty folks; we did our thing, had a blast, and then moved on. The box of extra booklets was banished to a dark corner in a garage until we found it years later. All that time, we could have been using this content for other things. We'd even recreated a few things in it all over again!

Marketing mostly becomes a chore when you know in your gut that you're not spending your time wisely. If you're doing something that isn't your forte or aren't using your assets to your advantage, you're working harder than you have to. Don't fall into this trap. Repurpose your content. Use what you've already created to connect with your readers in powerful ways. Talk about your book's characters—as you already are doing—but *record* yourself talking about them. Post a video to YouTube or to your website. Turn the video into an article. Turn the article into ten quotes to post to Twitter. Explain how you created the video in a blog post. Use the same content over and over again to work for you. You shouldn't be creating new stuff every week; you should be repurposing what you already have to creatively engage your audience.

Here are a few additional tips for making the marketing process more enjoyable, manageable, and purposeful:

- **Participate in the right marketing activities.** If you hate Facebook, forget about it. If you can't stand blogging, don't invest precious time and money forcing yourself to like it. On the flip side, if Instagram is your jam, dive in headfirst. Post there often, correspond with other people there, and make friends with strangers who might become potential readers.

- **Observe authors you admire.** One author we love is Chris Bohjalian. Check him out on Twitter and you'll see what we mean. He is constantly engaging his readers, thanking them for all they do, and encouraging them with his blog posts. Even if he isn't having a great time marketing his work, he certainly makes it seem like he is.

- **Avoid complaining, particularly on social media.** We, more than anyone else, understand that getting a book to press is hard work. But you aren't going to win any readers by complaining about your cover or a typo that somehow made it into your manuscript. Share your journey, yes. But keep the complaining to a very bare minimum.

- **Pace yourself.** You do not need to spend hours and hours every day on marketing efforts. That is a perfect recipe for burning out fast. Give yourself a goal of three or four hours per week to start. That is plenty.

- **Keep your sense of humor.** A lot of this publishing business is out of your control, and you're likely to give yourself a heart attack if you sweat the small stuff. Roll with the punches and smile. You're an author now, after all. Enjoy the prestige!

4

What does having an "internet presence" mean?

Your website, social media profiles, and online persona are the foundation of your platform. If one of your readers were to google your name or book title, you'd want them to find one of those avenues. But it doesn't end there.

Having a website will not automatically market your books, nor will having a Facebook page. As with anything in book marketing, any tools you invest will only be as good as your ability to use them effectively.

Being "present" on social media is not the same as being engaged. Being engaged is interacting with people—commenting, blogging, and continually talking with others about your book, your message, and your brand. Trust us when we say that people know the difference between a website that is parked and one that is active, a Twitter account that merely exists and one that has a thoughtful voice behind it. An Instagram account with two photos uploaded a year ago isn't marketing your book, nor is an occasional "Special Sale" post on Facebook following months of silence.

We know that every author's level of comfort on the internet is different. You might already have a huge social media following and be comfortable using your platform on a regular basis. Or you might be one of those people whose hands get sweaty at the thought of posting a status update on Facebook. The key is to remember that the internet is a tool to help your readers find you. Don't spend thousands of dollars or hours of precious time building a machine you can't maintain. Where do your readers hang out online, and who do they follow religiously? Who are the players already dominating the spaces where your readers are spending their time? Start there. Being online can be as simple as participating in forums, uploading articles to LinkedIn, pitching articles to *HuffPost*, and talking to other experts and popular authors online. With practice (and not a small amount of courage), you can create an internet presence that is both effective and comfortable for you.

Every so often we encounter an author who vehemently disregards the need to have an internet presence. Those authors are making their path to success much more difficult. If you have published a book, that book will wind up on the internet—reviewed on a website, mentioned on Twitter, or written about on a blog. Embrace the internet, and use it to engage your audience! You will find this journey much more enjoyable if you do.

Our secret is choosing no more than three platforms to be "present" on the internet. Think about the three platforms that you are most comfortable using regularly:

My Social Networks

1. _____

2. _____

3. _____

5

What general timeline should I follow?

There isn't one. You need to create a timeline yourself based on your marketing goals, potential events, and what would work best for your audience. Each book is unique, and as an author you are likely the best judge of when, where, and how your book should launch. However, below are a few guidelines that might help you with this process.

For our authors, it usually takes about nine months to go from submitting the manuscript to launching the book. This is about what you can expect as an indie author if you are using professional editors, designers, and printers. (Traditionally published books take, at a bare minimum, twice as long, and sometimes take several years to come out. For those authors, this timeline may not be applicable.)

The clock begins ticking when you sign your contract!

Nine months prior to launch:

- Submit your completed manuscript for content editing.

- Set your goals for publication! That is what the first part of this book is for.

- Engage in a back-and-forth with your editors. Take good notes, be very open to criticism, and allow yourself to try new things with style and content.

- Enjoy the editing process! All the work you do with your editing team serves to make your manuscript stronger.

Six months prior to launch (when your manuscript has been edited for content):

- Begin submitting your book (partials or the full manuscript) to beta readers and potential endorsers for testimonials and reviews. (Beta readers are people who form part of your ideal audience. Ideally, they are strangers or acquaintances; it can be hard to get honest, objective feedback from close friends and family. Reach out to book clubs, classrooms, businesses, or any other place where you might find people willing to read your book and review.)

- Keep detailed notes of who you have given your book to and what their feedback was. Be clear that you intend to use their feedback for promotional purposes. Most people are fine with this, but it's nice to make that clear from the forefront.

- Create the website and social media platforms you intend to use for author purposes.

- Begin engaging the community. For some, that means being a part of reading/writing events where you can take pictures, talk about your craft, and mention your forthcoming book. For others, it means engaging in live events held on social media. (On Twitter, this would be a "chat" with a hashtag that allows people to comment and interact with each other, and on Facebook this would mean commenting on a live video someone has posted in order to interact with their followers.) For others, it means taking part in networking events pertaining to your business and brand. For most, there will be a combination of many things to participate in. Choose what works for you.

- Begin building your email list.

Four months prior to launch:

- Submit your book for editorial reviews, if you choose to.

- Make some decisions about your launch party. What is it going to look like? What is your budget? What are some ways you can engage the community?

- Consider hiring a publicist to begin publicity work.

Three months prior to launch:

- Begin creating promotional materials or have someone create them for you.

- Set up your author pages on both Amazon and Goodreads.

- Consider setting up a blog tour. We devote all of chapter 31 to this topic!

- Secure the venue for your launch party.

- Consider giveaways of advance reader copies of your book to generate buzz on Goodreads and Amazon, as well as any other social media platforms relevant to your content.

- Contact your local bookstores or any other applicable venues for your content and ask them to host a signing for you.

- Make a decision about what distribution for your book is going to look like. If you are selling via your website, you will need to set up a purchase page.

One month prior to launch:

- Send out invites to your launch party.

- Begin taking and shipping preorders for your book via your website.

- Begin your "countdown" efforts on social media. Consider posting one endorsement per day; send out a weekly reminder via email saying, "Two weeks until the launch!";

reach out to the connections you've made over the last few months to invite them to read, endorse, and share your book.

Week of launch:

- Take a deep breath and be proud of how hard you have worked to get to this point!

- Enjoy your launch party and take in the celebration.

- Make sure to thank the people who have supported you throughout the process!

After the launch:

A new timeline begins at this point and only ends when you stop putting in the work. Marketing your book is no small task. This is where you get out into the community, share your gifts, work toward that earlier definition of success, and never lose sight of the fans you're creating.

Then reset: Measure what's working and what isn't. Add a check-in to your calendar to revisit your plan. Ask yourself, "What's changed?" Do you still care about the same things? What were the surprises of the last year marketing your book? What are your blind spots? Where should you focus more or less of your time?

Again, part of the joy of being an indie writer is owning your timeline. If these steps take you a full year, that is fine. If you have two launch parties, that is fine too. If you skip any of the above suggestions and decide later that you want to give it a try after all, go right ahead. It's certainly not a sprint, but it's not a marathon either; there is no finish line.

Visit wiseink.com/resources for a timeline!

6

What should my marketing budget be?

There is no way to definitively answer that question with a specific dollar amount. For some authors, money is no object. For others, every penny counts. Setting a budget for your book marketing requires reflection, conversations with family members you share expenses with, and finding the right balance of risk and reward.

The chart on the following page will help you align your marketing goals with your marketing budget:

Huge Budget ($10K+)	Medium Budget ($1,000–10,000)	Small Budget ($0–1,000)
• Hire a nationally recognized publicist to take care of all media (prices vary, but can range anywhere from five to eight thousand dollars).	• Have a publicist on retainer for a few hours of time, but take care of the press kit yourself.	• Forget the publicist. You can do it yourself!
• Travel nationally or internationally for writers' conferences and book events.	• Travel locally to writers' conferences and events, but skip anything that requires time off work or an overnight hotel stay.	• Plan to attend a few writers' conferences locally, but only if they are low- or no-cost.
• Acquire limitless marketing materials, such as galleys, swag, and table displays.	• Utilize strategic marketing materials such as galleys and swag, but maybe skip the large table displays.	• Create low-cost (but effective) marketing materials such as bookmarks. Forget printing galleys, but maybe have a nice sell sheet you can freely hand out to bookstores.
• Take out advertisements in major trade magazines.	• Skip advertisements in magazines, but maybe put some ads out in online publications.	• Skip advertisements altogether, but research blogs you could guest-post on in lieu of a blog tour.
• Take part in a highly publicized blog tour.	• Consider a blog tour.	
• Submit your book for any and all award opportunities.	• Enter a few strategic award opportunities.	• Skip the award opportunities, unless they are free to enter or really compelling for your book/genre.
• Have an awesome web designer make you an amazing website.	• Hire a web designer to make you an amazing website.	• Manage your own website via a free hosting site.
• Start weekly giveaways, both online and at events.	• Stage several strategic giveaways.	• Have very few giveaways.

The good news is that for every author success story built on a huge stack of hundred-dollar bills, there is another one hung from a shoestring budget. You do not need to spend thousands of dollars on marketing; however, those who do spend more money on marketing efforts have an advantage when it comes to getting the word out about their book. This boils down to time more than anything else. Creating marketing materials yourself, researching places to guest post, finding strategic people to read and review your work—all of this takes time. Almost all authors, indie or traditionally published, are working "real jobs" during the day, have family responsibilities, and would much rather be doing anything else than promoting their own book around the clock.

So as you consider your marketing budget, ask yourself, "How much time per week do I really have to spend marketing my work, and what is that time worth?"

What are your marketing "must-haves" (advanced reader copies, TV or radio appearances, online blog tours, table displays, etc.)? Think realistically about the things you simply know will work when it comes to marketing:

_____

_____

_____

_____

_____

_____

Total estimated cost for my "Must-Haves": _____

What are some "would-be-nice-to-have" marketing items for you?

_____

_____

_____

_____

_____

_____

_____

_____

_____

_____

_____

_____

_____

Total estimated cost for my "Would-Be-Nice-to-Haves": _____

Brainstorm creative ways you can use your network to get the marketing materials you want. Do you have a friend who's superb at graphic design? Can you partner with another author to share event space? Can you create swag to sell as opposed to give away?

_____

_____

_____

_____

_____

_____

_____

_____

_____

_____

Which sales tools are right for my book?

We are constantly telling authors that it's direct sales that will put the most money in their pockets, so they should sell direct anytime they are able. However, there is only one of you, and your reach is finite. So you'll want to use the tools that make the most sense for you and for your reader. Simply put, the right sales tools are the ones you're willing to master and use.

Keep in mind that, thanks to recent advances in technology, there are hundreds of tools to help you make a sale. The traditional sales tools of yore included partnering with bookstores and gift shops, signing books, advertising in national media outlets, and being featured in catalogs. Don't discount these options for your book, but keep in mind that there are tools available to you now that might not have been around a few years ago. There are new ways to reach your audience and get them excited about your content that you might not have thought of.

Before figuring out which tools are best for your audience and discovering a few nontraditional sales tools, answer the following questions:

Who will be purchasing my book? (This is often the same as your audience, but if your book is for children or makes a good gift, it might not.)

_____

_____

_____

_____

_____

_____

How does my audience purchase books? (Catalog? Online retailer? At live events?)

_____

_____

_____

_____

_____

How can I organically engage with my audience? (Newsletter? Email blast? Twitter? Courses?)

_____

_____

_____

_____

_____

_____

Where does my audience do their research?

_____

_____

_____

_____

_____

For fun, my ideal reader is likely to go to the following places online and in person (e.g. conventions, meetup groups, blogs, websites, online communities, and clubs):

_____

_____

_____

_____

These are the experts, public figures, social media profiles, and bloggers that my readers follow and trust:

_____

_____

_____

_____

_____

These are the hashtags important to my readers:

_____

_____

_____

While we absolutely love indie booksellers and highly recommend you work with your local bookstores in any and all ways possible, the truth is that Amazon is the most powerful indirect sales tool at your disposal. Here are our favorite ways to make Amazon work to your advantage:

- **Get as many reviews as possible before, during, and after your launch.** This is crucial. Remind your network through email—and ask a select group of friends and family to remind *their* networks—to review your book. When a reader shares a positive verbal review, ask them to post it on Amazon.

- **Make sure that your book's information is accurate and up to date.** Take advantage of Amazon's Author Central platform, where you can update your book's endorsements and add your photo, an extended biography, your website, and links to your social media accounts.

- **Plan a "blitz" to coincide with your launch.** Organize a group of people close to you to purchase and review your book on a specific date. Promote this date ahead of time and turn it into a virtual event. Not only will this set a deadline for some of your slacker friends, but it can also increase your odds of debuting high on sales charts.

Remember, content sells books. Social media is a powerful tool for sharing your content, and you should do so judiciously. Ideas include: uploading pictures of you at events to Facebook, asking timely questions on Twitter based on current events, pulling a quote from your book and posting it as an image to Instagram, and uploading how-to articles to LinkedIn.

However, try weaving your sales tools into areas where you already spend a lot of time so that you can spend less time building and more time marketing. Also add low-maintenance sales tools to your arsenal of resources—once they're created, upkeep is low and the return is high for helping more readers find you.

Examples of low-maintenance sales tools include:

1. An integrated shopping cart widget on your website

2. Offering free resources (e.g. checklists, templates, favorite tools) on your website in exchange for an email when someone visits your website or blog

3. Inviting attendees to subscribe to your email list at live events

4. A strategy to sell books at speaking engagements (e.g. a thoughtful presentation related to your book's topic, a dynamic table or booth, and the ability to accept credit cards)

5. A link to buy your book directly from your email signature

6. An affiliate arrangement with other authors or experts who promote your book on their websites

7. Advertising your book on websites, blogs, or podcasts that target your audience

8. A page in the back of your book that promotes you as a speaker (fiction authors, add a sentence to your copyright page or at the end of your bio that demonstrates your willingness to speak to groups or book clubs)

9. Amazon ads

How do I best reach my specific audience?

You will hear us say this over and over again, as it is one of the Ten Commandments of book publishing: Know thy audience!

Think carefully about your "ideal" reader. What do they do in their spare time? Where do they normally purchase things? Where do they go for information? And most importantly, what are unique and organic ways to get your book and message in front of them?

Hopefully, by the time you begin marketing your book, you will have already thought through these things carefully. Still, it's a good idea to refresh your memory. Also, be concrete in how you determine your market demographics. **Go deeper than the standard questions around gender, age, education, and geographic location. Those are just places to start.**

When describing your ideal reader, be specific with the details that matter, such as how much time they have to read, how they might use your book day-to-day, and how they generally make recommendations to others. Another thing to do is segment your readers into three specialized subgroups—communities that align with each reader's professional identities and personal aspirations. This helps you dig even deeper into the psychology of your readers in order to decide where it makes the most sense to spend your time. As an example: To market your business book, you might segment your readers into millennials and recent grads, aspiring entrepreneurs, and motivational speakers. If you've just published a sci-fi thriller, your subgroups might include fans of the popular sci-fi series *Black Mirror*, sci-fi writers who frequent fan-fiction sites, and people who attend conventions like WorldCon.

How does your ideal reader obtain information? Blogs? Magazines? Newspapers? Ads? What social media sites do they frequent? Be as specific as you can here. These are the places you will want to target in terms of marketing.

Where does your ideal reader shop? Think beyond bookstores. Are they frequent travelers? (Maybe they shop in airports a lot.) Do they have stores they tend to gravitate toward? Make a list of these places, and find people to connect with your book.

1. My ideal reader: (Use key words to describe them) _____

2. Social media sites they frequent: _____

3. Places they shop: _____

4. Organizations they support: _____

9

I want to make an impact with my book. Where do I start?

First of all, you rock. Impact is our favorite word at Wise Ink. We have found that authors who see their work as something that can positively impact lives are the ones who find the most success, both personally and professionally. The work you did with setting your goals was the first step in this.

Of course, the word *impact* carries different meanings, which is why we think it's wise to first define what impact means for you. Come up with one or two sentences or bullet points that specifically address the impact you're hoping to make with your book(s).

For example:

I want schools around the country to use my series as a teaching tool in their classrooms.
or
I want recent college graduates to have a tool that will help them navigate the job market.
or
I want my book to redefine how people view fantasy fiction and give them a completely new reading experience.

What does impact mean to me?

_____

_____

_____

_____

_____

_____

_____

As you can probably imagine, the definition of impact is personal and broad, and it is not easily measured. That shouldn't stop you from thinking about it, however. The impact you want to make will go hand in hand with your marketing efforts, and if you think about your marketing work in terms of impact instead of sales, you are bound to have a more fulfilling publishing experience.

Think about events, articles, or other ideas that will help you achieve your impact goals (and hopefully sell some books in the process!).

For example:

Create content for Teachers Pay Teachers based on the material in my book.
or
Create a YouTube video highlighting one or two tips from my book about landing a job after college.
or
Host a Reddit AMA (Ask Me Anything).

Marketing tactics that will help me make this impact are:

How important are endorsements before publication?

We think endorsements are important. Have you ever picked up a book at a bookstore because you liked the cover, even though you didn't know anything about it, and then saw that a writer you love said it was the best book of the year? Would that endorsement sway your decision to make the purchase? We're betting it could. It happens in all types of marketing—think celebrities who make millions of dollars endorsing products.

For authors, endorsements are probably even more important. If this is your first book and you don't have any name recognition, the truth is that your book is one of many in a saturated market. Endorsements add credibility. They're a way to impress your audience and prove to booksellers and potential buyers that you are the real deal. It is absolutely worth it to pursue getting endorsements before publication.

Securing endorsements doesn't have to be a difficult process. Simply make a list of the people in your life whose opinions on your book might carry some weight. If you are writing for the educational world, who are some teachers who might be willing to read and review your book? If you are writing for the business world, who in your network might know your work and be willing to give you a few words of praise? If you are writing fiction, which other writers could you give your completed manuscript to and ask for feedback? Do you know of any librarians, book bloggers, or bookstore owners?

If you are stuck, don't be shy about reaching out to friends and family and tapping into their networks. Ask kindly, and be willing to accept no for an answer. There is no harm in reaching out. We have found that many people are honored to be asked for input.

When you reach out for endorsements, it is okay to offer only part of the manuscript for review. A busy CEO might not have time to read your entire book, so maybe the first chapter would be sufficient for her to make a positive statement. We suggest that you offer the entire manuscript first; if time constraints are an issue, then offer a partial.

When you receive endorsements, keep careful track of them and be sure to thank the people who provided them. Let them know that you will be using their names and kind words to help spread the word about your book; however, be careful not to "tag" them on social media each time you mention their review. This can be very off-putting and disrespectful of that person's privacy.

People in my network I can contact for an endorsement:

_____

_____

_____

_____

List five to ten people outside your network (think big) who you will try to get a copy of your book to:

Remember, the best way to go about securing an endorsement is by being genuine. Here's an example of what we mean:

Dear Ms. So-and-So [business owner, educator, celebrity],

I have been following your blog, The Mindful Momma, for the past three years. I absolutely love the content you provide, and it's been invaluable for me as I've embarked on my motherhood journey. I especially love your recipe section. That is my go-to on busy nights, and I appreciate it!

The reason I'm reaching out is because I am a yoga teacher based out of the Twin Cities area and have just written my first book about the benefits of practicing meditation as a family. The book is called Breathe: A Guide for Family Meditation; *it is part information, part workbook, and part inspirational guide to help families get into this practice.*

My book will be published by Wise Ink Creative Publishing in the spring of 2019, and I am hoping to send you an advanced copy of the book for you to review and potentially endorse. It would be such an honor to have your support. In fact, I would be happy to offer a discount to your readers if you would like to mention the book on your blog.

Please let me know the format that you'd prefer to receive the book in. I can provide an uncorrected PDF immediately, or I can have an advanced copy sent to your home by the middle of next month.

I so appreciate your time and consideration. Thank you!

> *Sincerely,*
> *[your name and contact information]*

Should I do a Kickstarter or other crowdfunding campaign?

Kickstarter and other crowdfunding services are gaining popularity every single day, and you absolutely should consider launching a campaign if you are funding your book's publication independently.

Each platform is different, and we have seen success on both Kickstarter and Indiegogo as the two primary platforms for authors. The main difference between the two is that to receive your payment on Kickstarter, your project must be fully funded. (This means you need to set a realistic expectation; otherwise you risk losing the funding entirely.) Indiegogo, on the other hand, gives you the option to keep whatever you are awarded, regardless of whether you reach your goal or not.

On the following page are a few pros and cons to consider before jumping into a crowdfunding campaign:

Crowdfunding	
Pros	Cons
• You can obtain an audience you might not have otherwise been able to build before the launch. • You will receive a financial boost, either to repay yourself for your investment or to fund a future printing. • You can work fun, interesting "extras" into your campaign, which can be great marketing tools. • You will be selling those books directly, meaning any product you ship will be more profitable for you.	• New crowdfunding campaigns are posted every minute, and you will need to make yours unique and enticing so it will stand out. • The crowdfunding platform you choose will take a percentage of what you make. • You will need to be strategic with swag, which can be an added expense. • You will need to promote your campaign all the time, across all your networks. For some people, this is a turnoff from the whole idea of crowdfunding.

If you choose to do a crowdfunding campaign, here are a few tips to keep in mind to maximize your chances for success:

- **Create a compelling "story" to help personalize your campaign.** Take a look at the most successful crowdfunding campaigns for books. (We think the *Goodnight Stories for Rebel Girls* series is the gold standard for Kickstarter campaigns, and we are ridiculously proud of Wise Ink author Ara Elizabeth's campaign for *Rise and Shine*.) They all have a professional video that shares the larger vision for their books. Successful campaigns are good at convincing us that their vision is about more than just, "Donate to help me fund the great story I want to tell but can't afford to publish." Remember, people are wary of empty and superficial sales tactics. Invest in a great videographer, and make sure your video tells a powerful story about who you are and why your book matters.

- **Invest in the initial publishing steps first, then use the crowdfunding dollars to pay yourself back.** In order to have a wonderful, compelling video, you will need visuals. A book cover, for example. Possibly illustrations. In order to have those things, you will need to invest first, and use the crowdfunding dollars to pay yourself back or pay for the next step in the publishing process.

- **Make your rewards unique and strategic.** There are millions of ways to do this, so be sure the rewards you choose fit your book and your genre. Sure, a copy of your book, signed by you, is great. But what about a limited-edition canvas bag? A free PDF download of the manuscript? Some sort of thoughtful, unique piece of art? Again, look at successful Kickstarter campaigns and see what they do!

- **Promote, promote, promote.** One Facebook post about your Kickstarter campaign will not be enough. You will need to post several times a week, thanking people for their contributions and asking for more support. If this is not something you're willing to do, we don't recommend a crowdfunding campaign.

- **Be realistic about your goal.** Of course, it would be awesome to get $50,000 in backers for a $10,000 project. But putting your goal at $50,000 is not just difficult to attain; it also shows your audience you aren't sure what you are getting into. We suggest funding your indie book project yourself up until printing, and using a crowdfunding campaign to fund the printing of your book. That way, you have an easier-to-achieve financial goal, but also have the images and "story" that will help sell your campaign in the first place!

Visit wiseink.com for more crowdfunding tips and tricks in our 'author resources' section.

12

How important is social media, and which platform is best?

The short answer is that social media is supremely important. With so many people getting the vast majority of their information online, you truly are doing yourself a disservice by not engaging your audience or promoting your work on at least one social platform.

For some authors, this is simply a given. They already use social media, and tapping their established platforms to sell books is a no-brainer. But for many authors, this is not the case. Using social media to promote their work feels foreign. For some authors, social media is unintuitive and feels uncomfortable.

We suggest choosing one or two social media platforms to use consistently for book-selling efforts. (You are certainly welcome to use more, but remember that social media can be a huge time commitment. Be realistic about how much social media you will use.)

Another easy tip is to think about your average day and where you can incorporate something you already do—journaling, chatting about your favorite TV show, or snapping a picture of something interesting—into a social media platform that you're cool with. Don't make social media harder than it has it be. Take a few minutes every day to connect with readers about what you're writing, questions you're pondering, a quote that inspires you, a book you're reading, or a place you're going to be visiting soon—all these are easy ways to organically use social media. Your readers are busy and see marketing materials every day, so your personality is what will get their attention. Think about how to help your readers on social media—be a resource and you've offered a reason to keep coming back for more.

If you're trying to determine the right platform, keep these pros and cons in mind:

Facebook	
Pros	Cons
• Easy to use and boost posts • Most people who use the internet have Facebook accounts • Easy to join and interact with "groups" that contain your potential audience • A wonderful place to keep track of events and invite others to events you host • No limits to the length of your posts	• Hard to keep track of who is seeing your posts • Facebook is inundated with posts, groups, lists, etc. • Can be difficult to keep your personal and author pages separate • Facebook algorithms can result in your posts being made harder to see

LinkedIn	
Pros	Cons
• Perfect for authors with business books • A great place to network professionally	• Not great for fiction authors • Most people are not on LinkedIn

Twitter	
Pros	**Cons**
• Super easy to use • Twitter chats are a great way to engage your audience • Hosting a giveaway is easy • Great way to try to engage an endorser or pitch to a blogger	• Character limits can be challenging (though this has improved with the recently upped character limit) • Hard to get your tweet "noticed" • Most people are not on Twitter

Other social media sites to consider:

Goodreads: This is the social media site for readers. We recommend all authors have their book there and that they join the Goodreads Author Program. A wonderful place to connect with reading groups, too!

Instagram: This is ideal for people whose books are highly visual, authors who plan to document their writing journey in pictures, and authors whose marketing plans include targeting book reviewers and bloggers. Tip: check out the following hashtags on Instagram for an instant look at creative ways to take gorgeous photos of your book—#instabook, #bookstagram, #bibliophile, #booknerd, and #bookish.

Pinterest: A perfect site for blogging authors because you can pin your blog posts. Also good for authors with businesses, authors of inspirational and spiritual titles, and cookbook authors.

Tumblr: A splendid place for authors who have blogs and pictures and who enjoy posting a little bit of everything.

Social Media Dos and Don'ts

For every author who has found success with using social media to market their work, there is another who has found it exasperating. Social media, as with all aspects of marketing, is a delicate balance of content, message, and delivery. There is no silver bullet with social media, but we can say with certainty that begging or guilting people to buy your book will not work.

Here are our dos and don'ts to live by for social media:

Do	Don't
• Be intentional with your social media posts.	• Complain. It's tempting to vent when you're frustrated with sales, events, etc. But using social media to complain about how hard this whole publishing business is isn't going to win you any fans.
• Give yourself a goal to post something new once a week.	
• Let content drive your posts (for example, a new blog post, a new graphic, a new review).	• Over-post. There is a fine line between posting engaging content consistently and annoying people. If you post on any platform more than once per day, take a hard look at what you are posting and ask yourself what is really necessary and what is potentially clogging up your pages.
• Engage with your audience. That means responding to questions and thanking people—sincerely—for their comments and reviews.	
• Be honest and real. The authors who use social media well are the ones who aren't afraid to be genuine with their audience. People respond to authenticity.	• Tag people in your posts without their expressed permission. This is especially important when using photos. Everyone has different levels of comfort with social media—do not alienate people by disrespecting their privacy.
• Celebrate other writers in your genre. Sure, they are competition. But seeing yourself as part of a community that lifts others up is much more fulfilling than keeping yourself alone on your own island.	• Pay someone thousands of dollars if they promise to make you internet famous. These scams always result in disappointment.
• Follow and interact with other groups that align with your author brand and message.	• Post every single positive review that comes your way. Those will get old, fast!

Brainstorm a social media strategy that incorporates activities you enjoy doing and places where your readers spend a lot of time:

Platforms I will use:

Ideas for social media posts using quotes, photos, questions, and resources important to my audience:

_____

_____

_____

_____

_____

_____

_____

_____

_____

_____

_____

Visit wiseink.com for examples of great social media graphics!

Should I buy followers for my chosen social media platform?

In a word: No. In the current world, where social media is such a dominant way for a person or brand to present themselves, it's easy to fall into the trap of thinking that a lot of social media followers equals success. "If I have a thousand followers on Facebook, and even half of those people buy my book, that's five hundred books I've sold!"

If only it were that easy.

As you build your social media presence, you will likely be contacted by "social media experts" who want to "grow your followers." They usually do this through a direct message on your accounts and will charge a fee for this service. And yes, this sounds great, especially to someone just establishing their platform. However, there is a catch. They might be able to deliver on the promise of growing your followers, but more often than not, those new followers are fake accounts set up for this purpose. What is the point of having five thousand followers if none of them are real?

Your focus should be on organic connections. Twenty social media connections with people and organizations that consume your brand and might endorse your book are far more valuable than five hundred connections with people who won't. Is it work to cultivate authentic connection? Of course. Is it worth it? Absolutely.

Building an organic social media base takes time and patience. Use your time wisely by researching people and entities that complement your book and have large fan bases already set up. How can you reach out to them in a personal way? How can you uplift their brand while uplifting yours? If you can't connect personally, how can you use *their* social media platforms in a way that might benefit you?

Make a list of any and all social media personalities or organizations that you want to connect with and tap into in order to organically build *your* brand:

Social media personalities and organizations to connect with:

How should I use social media to market my book and brand?

If you haven't picked up a copy of Wise Ink's *Social Media Secrets for Authors*, you absolutely should. In that book you will find tips for using social media effectively. To access the PDF for free, visit wiseink.com.

Generally speaking, here are a few rules you should follow when using social media to market your book:

- Choose the platform(s) you are most comfortable with, and use them strategically. Don't create accounts for the sake of creating accounts. If you have no intention of blogging, don't start a blog. If your book doesn't lend itself to pictures, don't bother with Instagram. Be thoughtful about where you spend your time on social media.

- Don't get sucked into any social media platform. Twenty minutes a day is plenty of time.

- Use hashtags effectively. Twitter is a great place to use hashtags relevant to your content and engage with readers.

- Use visuals. Pictures are instant attention-grabbers, and so are simple graphics.

- Pay to "boost" your posts. Not *all* posts. But the ones that are especially engaging or important—boost those.

- Remember that not every post should be a plea for people to buy your book. Content sells your book best. Can you post articles about topics relevant to your genre? Can you ask a provocative question and engage people that way?

- Keep the personal and professional separate. This will likely be difficult, as the lines can blur in the publishing world. But keep in mind that, as an author and a public figure, you should be careful about putting too much of your information out there.

- Use social media to tell your story and personalize the voice behind your content. Don't overthink your posts. Be you. Social media is absolutely about quality more than quantity. A reflective and thoughtful post beats a thousand posts where your readers aren't learning more about who you are and what matters to you.

Brainstorm your favorite voices on social media. Think about why you respect their presence. What do you most admire about them and why? Why do you pay attention to these folks?

Here are a few more suggestions for using social media to promote your book. Keep in mind that each author and genre is different, so what works for one author might not work for another.

- Create a contest on Instagram or Facebook, and have the participants do more than retweet or "like" a post. Prompt them to leave a comment, share a favorite resource, or tag a friend. Engaging potential readers is the key, so how can you get readers to tell you more about themselves? How can you make it so you can personally contact all the entrants of the contest and invite them to follow you on social media or purchase your book at a discount?

- Launch a Giveaway. It can be really effective, but it will require digging on your part. Can you partner with other authors of your genre for a group giveaway? Can you partner with an organization to have them either promote or endorse your book?

- Share Value: Resources, Quotes, Tools. We cannot state this enough: let content sell your book. Instead of using social media to get your book in front of people, use it as a tool to communicate your big picture. As your fanbase grows organically, so will the people interested in what you have to say.

Use other authors as inspiration. The possibilities are endless. Write down the ideas you've seen used by other authors that you'd be willing to try. Then choose one and create a strategy around it.

Social Media Personality	Platforms Used	How They Effectively Engage Users	Ideas for Me

15

How important is an email list, and how often should I be emailing the people on it?

When it comes to email marketing, two things are true. First, for most authors, an email list is crucial. And second, most authors do not compile an email list soon enough, if at all.

We cannot possibly overstate how valuable your email list is. It is far more valuable than your Facebook likes and LinkedIn connections, and it's far more potent than a book trailer or blog tour.

Only a fraction of your social media followers will see any given post. However, unless your message ends up in the spam folder, almost all the people on your email list will at least read the subject line.

Let's frame it another way: how many people do you know who either aren't on a certain social media platform, or don't use it much? We are guessing a large number. Now, how many people do you know who don't use email on a daily basis? We are guessing far fewer.

Email is one of the most effective ways you will engage your platform. This means you need to carefully cultivate this email list. Here's how you do that:

- **Use a service to manage your mail list.** We like MailChimp, but there are others. Yes, it's a big pain to transfer emails from your personal account to a service. However, sending emails from MailChimp is a breeze, looks very slick and professional, and gives people the chance to opt out. (It always stinks when someone opts out of receiving your emails, but it is better than angering them with unwanted emails.) You will also be able to manage your lists better, see how many people are opening and reading your emails, and determine how effective a certain campaign is.

- **Grow your list at events.** Bring an email signup sheet to every event you go to. Encourage people to sign up, and consider offering them a reward—such as a free chapter or a Jolly Rancher—for doing so.

- **Make it part of your sales routine.** Be diligent about adding people to your email list when they purchase directly from you.

- **Do not over-email.** Once per month is plenty. Make sure your content is relevant and interesting. Too many emails are the worst. Don't be spammy.

- **Don't make your emails about you.** Emails asking people to buy your book are not a good idea. Yes, you can send a monthly email that contains a cool promotion, updates about your latest events, or news about a partnership; however, free, reader-centric content works wonders. The less you sell your book and the more you inundate your reader with tips, tools, ideas, or a cool story, the more successful you will be at selling more books. Remember: quality over quantity.

- **Add an opt-in box to your website.** Usually, this is a pop-up box that you can add yourself (or have your web designer add).

- **Seek your readers, not everyone.** Not everyone belongs on your list, so don't force people who are not prospective buyers to opt in. Noisetrade and Netgalley are two places where you can allow people to download your book (for free) in exchange for their email address and the potential for a review. This is a nice way of making sure that the emails you are collecting are from people who are genuinely interested in your work.

If you are emailing your list monthly, which is more than enough, that means you have twelve opportunities to engage people and market your book. Here are a few ways you can utilize your email list in productive (and not annoying) ways.

- **A monthly author newsletter.** Don't overthink this. A quick check-in about the events you have coming up, a few pictures from past events, and maybe any news surrounding the book is plenty. Incorporate something that's reader-centric, not you-centric—a fan photo favorite, an inspirational quote, or a free resource.

- **A favorite blog post or supplemental material.** Did you write a blog you'd like to share in an email? Did you create a Q&A that could be shared with your audience? An email is a useful way to share that.

- **A promotion.** Promotions should be timely and relevant. Before you get too caught up in making the perfect promotion, think about which promotions catch *your* eye. Free shipping? BOGO? A signed copy? A donation of an amount of proceeds to a favorite charity?

- **A holiday deal.** Sure, this is the same as a promotion. But if there is a holiday that is particularly relevant to your book, or you are partnering with other brands as part of a gift set, this is good news to share.

- **Recommended resources and links to other experts and authors.** We believe strongly that authors who see other authors in their genre as competition are putting themselves at a disadvantage. Sure, you are "competing" for readers, but readers of your genre are likely always on the hunt for new books in a similar vein. Make friends with other authors, and share their information in your newsletter if it is relevant to your readers. These are the types of partnerships that can lead to wonderful, intangible returns.

Brainstorm ideas for engaging your email list. Be specific and creative! If you can't think of more than a few items, that is okay. Consider a mailing every two months, or even once per quarter.

16

Does it matter if there is a similar book to mine on the market?

Nope. When you find yourself in this situation, because you will, you have two options: you can either sulk and hope nobody makes any comparisons between your book and someone else's, or you can proactively use similar books to expand connections and boost your own brand. You can guess what our choice would be.

In other words, use competition to your advantage. Boldly mention competitive books and highlight why your book is different. Tap into communities that read your competition. Get familiar with how competitive books are being marketed and to whom.

Use the chart on the next page to research competitive titles and highlight strengths and weaknesses.

Now is your opportunity to reach out to fellow authors. Follow them on Twitter, engage them on Instagram, and send them a personal email noting the similarities in your books with the hope that you can work together to cross-promote.

Title	Author	Social Media/Contact	Strengths	Weaknesses

What *exactly* do I need to know about my competition?

Before we answer this question, let's ask what's probably a more important question: what makes another book your competition?

Even if you think your book is the only one like it on the market, competitive books probably exist. A book can be your competition if it serves the same audience as yours, if it touches on the same topic, if it's primarily sold through the same channels, or if it shares a special format with your book. In other words, content is not the only way a book can be your competition. For example, if your book is a photography book, printed in full color, and designed to cater to history buffs, your competitive books include other coffee table books, perhaps gift books, and books that touch on the subject matter of your photos.

In other words, competition for this book isn't just other photography books with similar photos. It's any book that could potentially sit next to it on a shelf in the bookstore. And this is a good thing. You don't want to be the lone voice shouting to the masses. Competition means there's a market for your book. Your readers are already convinced they enjoy, or even *need*, the kinds of books you like to write. That's why we encourage you to see other authors as allies, not competition.

Researching your competition will provide powerful insights about your audience. What should your competitive research reveal?

- Who are the major players? Which authors are the most trusted, the most entertaining, and the most followed? Who is exceeding expectations through offering the most value, and how are they doing it (e.g. through offering a high volume of content, free content, low-cost content, well-designed content)? How are they standing out?

- On average, what products do competitive authors offer? How do they look? How are they marketed and promoted?

- How do readers interact with these competitive authors? Where are they purchasing these books?

- What are the most creative selling strategies of your competition? Are they primarily using digital marketing, email marketing, social media, or a combination? How do they network and where? What do their social media profiles look like?

We've found that authors should research their competition in three major spaces:

1. **The speaking circuit.** Chances are, as a speaker you are tapping into your local rotaries, professional development organizations, and libraries for potential speaking gigs. If your topic is similar to others' topics, or if there's a speaker who is the go-to for your particular topic, consider this excellent intel. It's time to get creative in how you pitch your presentation in a way that sets you apart. Here's where your brand matters and where your stories, experiences, and personality can drive the methods you use to create talks that are unique. What are the top questions you're asked as an author and expert? What was your writing experience like? What are your favorite learned lessons? Do you know shortcuts or tips that will make the audience happier or smarter? Start there. In short, make your presentation different. That way organizers

aren't choosing between two like options, but making room for a presentation that fits and is distinct.

2. **The book festival circuit.** Of course, we at Wise Ink love book festivals. A room filled with authors, publishers, and readers—sign us up! The upside of getting a table at a book festival is that these are your people, and you'll hopefully make valuable connections. These are also perfect places to observe your competition and audience up close, gather resources, ask for advice, and collect ideas. The potential downside to book festivals is that they're one of few places your book will be compared to tons of other books at one time, in an overwhelming and often incredibly crowded setting. While we definitely recommend participating in book festivals, we suggest a few ways to minimize the "competitive" nature of them:

    - Draw people to your table in a purposeful way. A bowl of candy is always nice, but what else can you do to get people to stop, talk, ask questions, and purchase your book? How can you sell more than one book at a time to a distracted but interested customer?

    - Know ahead of time the buzzwords that readers are drawn to and use them in your elevator pitch. Offer something for free: tip sheets, coloring pages for children, recipe cards, and tchotchkes (mugs, temporary tattoos, T-shirts, stickers, or pens) are a few things we've seen work really well.

    - Choose your book festivals carefully. Going to a mostly-fiction book festival isn't usually wise for a nonfiction author, and vice versa. Make sure you get a feel for how well-attended a festival or conference is before purchasing a booth, and pay attention to where your table will be placed. Try to have a booth close to entrances, the snack or coffee area, or open areas where there's likely to be a good amount of traffic.

    - Be strategic with your sales and packaging. Can you offer a really enticing discount or gift-wrapping?

- Use your time wisely. Don't sit behind your table and hope people come to you—go out to them. Network with other authors; they are potential customers too.

3. **Social media.** We're guessing that your top competitors are killing it on at least one social media platform. Even if you decide that it isn't your thing, you should still know where your readers are hanging out on social media and who they are paying attention to. Through this research you'll discover popular hashtags, online chats, keywords, and the platforms your readers are drawn to. You'll also discover potential allies and, most important, selling strategies that work the best for your genre using social media.

18

How do I get reviews for my book?

Before we talk about *how* to get reviews, let's talk about *why* they are important. Of course, by now you know that because so much of our purchasing is done online and the market is saturated with books of all genres, your book must stand out. One way to do that is to have a bounty of stellar reviews, so when people discover your book they know others have read it and agree that it's wonderful.

Another reason reviews are important has to do with algorithms. Although Amazon is always tweaking the way it chooses to display books and does not release the details of its algorithm to the public, one of the factors it takes into account is the number of reviews. At one point, authors figured out that books with more than fifty reviews were being suggested on the pages of other books of a similar genre. Having your book placed next to a bestseller of a similar genre has the potential to do wonders for your sales. Whether or not this exact metric is still true as you're reading this, Amazon will surely still be taking the number of reviews a book has into account.

Reviews are also important because they give you a chance to engage with your audience. As an indie writer, you have the potential to thank people who take the time to review your work. You can also offer them special promotions or discounts.

Do you absolutely need to allot several hours per day to getting reviews for your book? No. Is it worthwhile to make this a high priority? Yes.

There are two types of reviews that are important for you as an author.

1. **Editorial Reviews.** Editorial reviews come from established review sites, magazines, or newspapers, and can be really good for your marketing efforts. Some authors—especially those with great publicists—are able to land reviews in trade magazines and newspapers, but these are hard to come by for indie authors. There are several places that offer editorial reviews of self-published works for a significant fee:

   - *Kirkus*
   - *Self Publishing Review (SPR)*
   - *IndieReader*
   - *Clarion*

Pros	Cons
• Depending on the source, an editorial review can carry a lot of weight.	• As an indie author, most editorial reviews will cost money, and they are not guaranteed to be positive. Nothing feels worse than paying someone a few hundred dollars to tell you that your book is terrible.
• When you pay for an editorial review, you usually have the option of keeping this review from being posted.	• Like any marketing effort, positive editorial reviews don't guarantee book sales.
• You can use editorial reviews for all of your marketing efforts—for excerpts on the book cover, sell sheets, press releases, and swag, as well as your Amazon author page.	• While some editorial reviewers, *Kirkus* especially, are well-known in the book industry, most potential buyers aren't going to recognize any source short of the *New York Times Book Review*.
• When you approach bookstores about signings or events, having positive editorial reviews behind you will be a bonus for receiving their support.	

2. General Reviews. These are a few places that collect reviews from general readers:

- Amazon
- Goodreads
- LibraryThing
- Netgalley (You must pay for placement on this site, and subscribers download a free ebook in exchange for an honest review.)

Pros	Cons
• With the exception of Netgalley, you will not pay for a general review. • You can still use general reviews in marketing materials, even though they don't carry the weight that an editorial review does. • You can use reviews as a way of connecting to your audience. Thank them for their reviews directly on Amazon, and you might make some lasting relationships!	• It can be time-consuming to accumulate a large number of general reviews; it often includes a lot of nudges to friends and family to "Please review my book on Amazon!" People outside the publishing world don't understand how important reviews are for indie authors—it is your job to educate them! • It is possible to search "top reviewers" on Amazon and approach them directly about reviewing your book, but this will be time consuming. If reviews are supremely important to you—as they should be—then it might be a good use of your time to search these people out and contact them individually.

Before spending money on editorial reviews or a service such as Netgalley, take a look at your goals. Good reviews rarely turn books into bestsellers. However, they do strategically expand audiences.

One last thing about reviews—there will be negative ones. They might come from strangers, they might come from those editorial sites that you paid money for, and they might even come from people who dislike you personally. Negative reviews, like positive reviews, are part of this business. People who've never written a book before will post unconstructive comments on Amazon and Goodreads that they wouldn't dream of saying to your face.

Do your best to treat a negative review as an opportunity to grow as a writer. It's easy to focus all your energy on the negative reviews—don't fall into this trap. There's not a single person on the planet that you should allow to rock your confidence or diminish the passion you have for your book. No book that has many reviews from strangers is going to get universally positive feedback.

Goals for gaining reviews for my book:

_____

_____

_____

_____

_____

_____

_____

_____

_____

_____

Review sites and strategies that make the most sense for me:

_____

_____

_____

_____

_____

_____

_____

_____

_____

_____

_____

_____

_____

Do I need to print
Advanced Reader Copies (ARCs)?

You don't *need* to print ARCs. But maybe you should. ARCs are a tool for getting early reviews and key endorsements before your official launch. They're also a smart way to generate buzz for your book in the weeks and months leading up to your launch. You can send them with a sell sheet or press release to booksellers, editorial review sites/magazines, blogs, newspapers, influencers in your field, and potential endorsers.

To figure out whether or not an ARC printing is right for you, answer the following questions:

- Do you have the funds to spend on the extra printing?

- Do you have a list of endorsers, reviewers, or corporations that could help increase prelaunch buzz or presales?

- Can you find a way of getting the recipients of your ARCs to give useful endorsements or leave reviews and post their support for your upcoming launch on social media?

If the answer to all of those questions is yes, then you might consider printing at least twenty-five advanced reader copies.

Brainstorm ways printing ARCs might benefit you. Who could you send them to? How will you use them for advanced publicity and media coverage?

Benefits of printing ARCs:

_____

_____

_____

_____

I will send my ARCs to:

_____

_____

_____

_____

_____

20

How do I get my book sponsored?

Having a book paid for by an organization is a dream for many indie authors. In this scenario, your book's message resonates with an organization so much that they invest in making that book a part of their own marketing materials or curriculum. Companies are often willing to pay for a custom printing, usually including their company logo or some other signifier on the cover.

Sponsorships are not easy to come by, and for good reason. If you're an indie author, you know how much it costs to print and sell your book. An organization would only be willing to do this for your book if they were sure that it would be a good business strategy for them. For this reason, there is no formula for getting your book sponsored. Most of the time, it is a matter of getting your book and your message into the right person's hands at the right time.

That said, sponsorships are certainly worth pursuing for some books—books written to serve a marginalized community, books that complement a particular cause or nonprofit, and books that can be marketed to corporate entities that hire trainers and professional speakers. Below is a guide to help you determine if your book is a good fit for a potential sponsor.

Write down your book's mission statement.

Now, write down the names of three to four organizations that have similar mission statements, have heard your message, or have purchased your book in the past.

Once you have identified a few organizations, do diligent research. Who are the key decision-makers that might handle sponsorship opportunities?

What are upcoming events and fundraisers that these organizations have on their calendars that your book and message might be valuable for?

While you can certainly try cold-calling (or emailing) an organization about sponsoring your book, we wouldn't recommend it. Instead, see if you can schedule a coffee or in-person meeting with a key stakeholder. Once your meeting is scheduled, bring a copy of your book and discuss the options in person. Maybe you can offer a speaking series to go along with your sponsored printing, or maybe the organization can host a launch event. Having a corporate sponsor is a big commitment on both your parts, and will hopefully lead to a lasting relationship. Nurture that relationship carefully.

Should I have a book launch party? (And how do I do that?)

Yes! Why wouldn't you have a party to celebrate the tremendous accomplishment of publishing a book?

The definition of the term "launch party" varies from author to author. For some authors, a launch party is a given. Even before the book has been edited, they already have a venue booked and an event planner staffed. If that is you, wonderful!

For other authors, the thought of a launch party is daunting. A party to celebrate *you*? Let's be honest, we authors are mostly introverts by nature—so if this is you, don't fret.

Yes, you do need a launch party. And no, it doesn't have to be painful.

Our main piece of advice for authors throwing a launch party is to make it comfortable. No stress allowed. Set the date for your event a month out from when you expect books to arrive so that a snag at the printer won't make you pull your hair out hoping to still get books on time.

If you are comfortable throwing yourself a catered event with a red carpet and paparazzi, do that. If you are a backyard BBQ kind of person, go for it. If you have a book that lends itself to a specific event or venue, find a way to make that happen for you. There are no limits to what your launch party can be, so think outside the box and do something fun and memorable.

One common mistake authors make is believing that their book launch party should be at a bookstore. While having your launch party at your favorite local bookstore is a wonderful way to create a lasting partnership with that store and bring in business for them, the truth of the matter is that they will take around 40 percent or more of your proceeds, even though you will do almost all of the work to draw the audience. Think about how many books you believe you can sell at the party; is losing half of those proceeds worth using the space, or would that money be better spent in other places? We suggest having your launch party at a location that allows you to keep 100 percent of your proceeds, and saving the bookstore events for your "tour" in the months after your book comes out.

Here are our dos and don'ts for hosting your own book launch:

Do	Don't
• Presell tickets to your event, and have that presale cost include the cost of one book. That way people can come to the event and have a book already signed and ready to go, and you won't have to spend time dealing with transactions.	• Forget to plan how you will handle book sales. Purchase a Square or other device to process credit cards beforehand and have everything set up for purchase on the big day. Give your phone and a cash box (with plenty of change) to someone you trust and make them handle all transactions—you're going to be too busy mingling with guests to worry about managing money.

Do	Don't
• Create an event that will attract your local community. Can you invite a guest speaker with local name recognition? A band? Does your book lend itself to outside readers or thought leaders? Can you offer another small business the chance to showcase their product or service? The more you encourage the public to support your launch event, the better chance you have of attracting a larger crowd.	• Be afraid to speak at your launch. In fact, people will want to hear about your book, the process it took to be published, and the ups and downs that led to this point. Thank the people who've supported you at the very least!
• Have a reasonable budget. There is no need to host an open bar and have catered food and pay a hefty rental fee to a facility if that is not financially feasible for you. Even if your budget is $100, you can create an event that is both memorable and profitable.	• Overspend. If you love event planning, you know that things can get very expensive very fast. You have already put a lot of time and money into your book—there is no need to go into debt for the first of your many book events.
• Consider having a "special." Maybe you have a discount for multiple books so that attendees can give a copy of the book to a friend or two. (This can be a great plan around the holidays!) Maybe you have stationery printed out that you sell as a bundle with your book. Maybe you have matching tote bags available for people who buy five or more books. The list is endless.	• Forget to have a sign-in sheet to capture your guests' email addresses. Send an email the next day (or shortly thereafter) thanking them for coming, and then send a follow-up email expressing your appreciation and containing a reminder to write a book review on Goodreads and Amazon.
• Create a Facebook event for your launch about a month prior. Facebook events can get strangers to come to events nearby they might not have known about. Encourage your friends to share the event on Facebook, and thank them when they do.	• Forget to photograph the event and encourage people to do the same. Share a special hashtag that people can use when they post their pictures. Consider a "photo-booth section" where people hold up a copy of your book and have a photo taken with it. Photos of your event are a wonderful marketing tool to use for weeks and months after the event.

My list of launch party ideas:

_____

_____

_____

_____

_____

_____

_____

_____

_____

_____

_____

_____

_____

_____

22

Should I hire a publicist?

Maybe. Publicists are expensive. If you have a small marketing budget, spending thousands (yes, thousands) of dollars on a publicist probably won't make financial sense for you. You absolutely do not need a publicist to have a successful journey as an author, indie or otherwise.

Before going into the pros and cons of hiring a publicist, keep in mind that hiring a publicist in no way guarantees that your book will sell more copies. This is so important that we are going to repeat it in bold: **hiring a publicist does not guarantee sales of your book.** In fact, nothing guarantees sales of your book. If only it were as easy as throwing money at someone to instantly transform your book into a national phenomenon!

That said, a publicist, by trade, will have far more connections than you to assist with getting the message out about your book. A good publicist can write effective press releases with relevant news angles and has experience pitching authors to the appropriate media outlets. The right publicist will also have connections you might not know you need and might be able to expand your audience in ways you didn't realize were possible.

If you are in the market for a publicist, look for the following things:

- **Experience in the book world.** A good publicist should be able to show you a track record of success in getting authors exposure—bonus points if they can prove they have experience getting exposure for authors in your genre. A publicist who has twenty years in corporate publicity isn't going to do much for a fantasy fiction author.

- **Connections to your local market.** Unless you already have a huge national fanbase, we suggest you start local and work your way out in terms of getting yourself noticed. (Yes, we would all love a spot on the *Today Show* the week we publish our first book—but that is not going to happen, not without the help of an obscenely expensive publicist and a very lucky break. What *could* happen, however, is a spot on local radio, which you can record and use for future marketing efforts.)

- **Tenacity.** How willing are they to follow up on the connections you are hoping to make with your publicity efforts? How many authors are they handling at one time, and how quickly are they able to respond to requests? Hiring a publicist is an investment, and you need to be sure you get your money's worth.

- **Realism.** If a publicist promises you the moon, run the other direction. A publicist's job is to pitch you as best they can, but at the end of the day, it's not up to them when and where your book is picked up. Don't get us wrong—a publicist should have plenty of enthusiasm for your project, and it should show in how they talk to you about it. But there are simply no guarantees.

Important note: Hiring a publicist is not the end of the story. A publicist is not a mind reader, nor are they intimately connected to your audience like you are. When you talk to publicists about your book, you cannot simply say, "I don't know what I want or don't want, just get me anything!" That strategy is going to waste your publicist's time and your money.

Things to keep in mind in order to have a successful relationship with your publicist:

1. **Give them direction.** Tell them precisely how you are measuring success with publicity, and quantify it with numbers before you sign a contract. See the template below.

Publicity Strategy Template	
Two Radio Interviews	
Station/Program 1	
Station/Program 2	
Placement in three trade magazines	
Magazine 1	
Magazine 2	
Magazine 3	
One television appearance	
Local TV show 1	
National TV show 1	
Two event placements	
Event 1	
Event 2	

2. **Keep your goals in mind.** Everything goes back to those definitions of success you wrote down in chapter 1. If a publicist connects you with an opportunity that sounds great on paper but doesn't serve your goals, redirect their focus. Don't compare yourself to other authors and *their* definitions of success. Work toward *your* goals.

3. **Save everything.** One mistake authors tend to make is forgetting to keep all of their media appearances. Interviews and articles aren't always stored online forever, but any press about you and your book will be wonderful marketing tools months and years out.

Before venturing out and hiring a publicist, answer these questions as honestly as possible:

1. Do I have the time and patience to publicize my own work?

2. Do I have connections to local media outlets that I can tap into myself?

3. Do I have a strong network of supporters who will happily and consistently spread the word about my book?

If you answer yes to any of those questions, don't hire a publicist right away. Start on your own, and if six months down the line you change your mind or your connections dry up, revisit hiring help.

If the answer is no to all three of those questions, consider hiring a publicist. Keep in mind there is no need to sink a fortune into publicity. Depending on your budget, consider hiring a newbie publicist willing to do groundwork at a fraction of the cost. Sometimes, publicists breaking into the field have new, fresh eyes that can do wonders for an author's brand. One place to see if there are any publicists out there you are willing to take a chance on is Guru.com.

Any affiliation you have with a publication or media outlet is one you should pursue. Brainstorm all the different outlets you have connections to, so you can either pursue them yourself or give them to your publicist to pursue on your behalf.

Hometown	Education	Current Residence
(e.g. newspapers, publications, and media events in the area where you grew up)	(e.g. newspapers, publications, and media events in the area where you went to school)	(e.g. newspapers, publications, and media events in the area where you currently reside)

Outline your ideas for publicity. We like to organize them by the amount of effort they require. Highlight the items that will require assistance. Be specific—you can use this as a checklist for you or your publicist.

Small Effort (e.g. blog placements, small local publications where you have contacts, small local businesses where you believe you'll have no trouble securing a signing or event, etc.):

Medium Effort (e.g. bookstore signings; larger events where you might have to pitch yourself as a keynote speaker or guest author; large city newspapers, TV shows, or literary publications; etc.):

Large Effort (e.g. national TV shows, pitching to large corporations where you don't have contacts, being a guest contributor to a major national magazine that is relevant to your work, etc.)

_____

_____

_____

_____

_____

_____

It is easy to become overwhelmed when doing publicity yourself—so much to do, so much uncertainty, and so few ways to really quantify if your publicity efforts are translating into actual sales. We get it. With publicity, as with everything else in the publishing journey, keep in mind that you are running a marathon, not a sprint. Don't lose hope if your publicity efforts don't result in superstardom. We have found that the real reward in publishing comes from interacting with your readers, anyway.

What is a media kit, and how do I create one?

Media kits are collections of marketing materials you can use for your book. Press releases, sell sheets, media interviews, and links for purchase are usually included in media kits. Do you need a media kit? Probably.

If you have hired a publicist, they should be putting together a media kit for you. Work with them to make that happen. If you haven't (see the previous chapter if you aren't sure you need one), the thought of putting together a media kit can be overwhelming. Don't stress about it. Think of putting together a media kit in the same way you would approach organizing a closet: it might be a little time-consuming, but it's totally worth the effort.

Press release

A press release is a short article created to connect your book with relevant news that can be shared with reporters and news outlets. What's considered "news" is debatable. Your launch, for example, is news. An award win is news. An enhanced second edition of your book is news. However, your press release is more likely to gain traction and capture the attention of a reporter if you can connect it to something more general, timely, and interesting to a large audience. Research trending news topics. Also, factor in holidays and important dates that are likely to be covered that your book can be tied to. In general, know the selling points that are likely to grab a reporter's attention and then connect them to a current news topic. Often, you as the author are more interesting to a reporter than your book.

Keep in mind that press releases are written in the third person and are something that a reporter could in theory expand into an enhanced article. Things to include in your one-page press release are:

- A small image of your book cover
- Page count, format, ISBN, and purchasing information
- One or two endorsements
- A brief author bio
- Well-written content, in the third person, announcing your news

Sell sheet

Often, the sell sheet and the press release are used interchangeably, but there are important differences in these two documents. Often the sell sheet is a jazzed-up version of the press release. Sell sheets also more directly sell your book and aren't designed to be objective like a press release. The content on a sell sheet might be less formal, and the images and graphics might be more creative. You might include your author headshot as well as a coupon on the bottom for the purchase of your book. Some sell sheets do not include all the details for purchase, such as your ISBN and page count, but rather feature a link to your website and contact information. We suggest creating a sell sheet that advertises your book to potential buyers and informs them of the innovative ways you are connecting with your audience.

Your author bio

Part of a traditional author media kit is a well-written, one-page bio, along with a professional headshot. Be sure to include the inspiration for writing your book, relevant quotes, and information that describes why you were the perfect person to write this particular book. This bio should be written in third person.

Possible interview questions

An optional component of your author media kit is a list of interview questions and answers. This helps make a reporter's job easier. They don't have to come up with questions to ask you—you've already done the work for them. To create these questions and answers, tap into the mind of your audience and come up with a list of the top questions you know from experience readers have about you, your book, and your mission.

Book excerpt

If your book is fiction, choose an excerpt of no more than three pages to illustrate what it's all about. We know this is a difficult task. If you are struggling to come up with the perfect excerpt, pick the first chapter or the first three pages, whichever is shorter. If your book is nonfiction, include the table of contents with your excerpt.

Testimonials

If possible, collect a page of testimonials for your book. Reviews from select fans are okay if you don't have any editorial reviews, but endorsements from publications, experts, and authors are much better.

Possible blog posts or additional content

Can you create supplemental material to add to your media kit, such as a study guide or book club discussion page? Consider a page of additional content that might have been left out of the book for one reason or another.

Keep in mind that you likely won't be asked for your entire media kit. The purpose of creating one, particularly at launch time, is to make it easy for people in the media to cover your launch. Most outlets will have neither the time nor the interest to read your book cover-to-cover before reporting on it, so you will be much easier to write about if you've done a lot of the legwork for the reporter or blogger.

While having a professionally designed media kit is an option, it is also very possible to do all of this work yourself and save quite a bit of money. It is the content that will sell your media kit (and you!) the best.

Use this area to brainstorm the contents of your media kit. (You can download the PDF version of the media kit for this book at wiseink.com.)

Media kit contents:

_____

_____

_____

_____

_____

_____

_____

_____

_____

_____

24

What is the difference between a sell sheet and a press release, and how do I use them?

First off, do you even need a sell sheet or a press release? See the previous chapter if you aren't sure. The answer is probably. Sell sheets and press releases are useful tools to tell the world about your book without having to summarize in an email or give multiple copies of your book away for free to key endorsers or media.

A press release is a one-pager that announces news about your book. The text is concise and detailed, something a journalist could, in theory, develop into a lengthier newspaper or magazine article. A press release is simple, often including an image of your book cover and perhaps an author headshot or an award seal. The majority of a press release is text, and also includes specifics about your book (format, page count, trim size) and its distribution channels. Press releases are distributed to media outlets and, on occasion, bookstores.

A sell sheet is also only one page. It displays all of your book's key details, but it is different from a press release in that it doesn't highlight book news. A sell sheet is mostly book data—sales price, page count, trim size, a brief synopsis, key endorsements, and distribution information. Sell sheets are tools to attract sales from bookstores, gift shops, or buyers interested purchasing your book in bulk. Having a printed version will come in handy, but attaching an electronic version to an email along with an excerpt works too. Sell sheets also make perfect handouts at events where you have an author table.

For an example of a sell sheet and press release, visit the 'author resources' page at wiseink.com

25

What's the right number of copies to print for my first run?

Notice that the question isn't "How many books should I print?" We want you to think beyond that. Your goal should be to have more than one print run. Hopefully, your long-term plan is to have a steady stream of books selling for years.

Unfortunately, at the point most authors are ready to make this decision, they are juggling quite a few different factors—their incurred costs, timeline, and forthcoming marketing events, to name a few. So don't wait until the last minute to start thinking about your printing plan. Start thinking about your print quantity from the moment you decide to self-publish.

How many books you want to print is a business and marketing decision, not an emotional one, and you should make that decision wearing your entrepreneurial hat, not your writer hat. The answer basically comes down to: how many books can you realistically sell in the first twelve to eighteen months of your book's release? Here's where you get real about your sales strategies. How are you going to drive your sales week-to-week and month-to-month? When authors wait too long to begin thinking about this, they are more likely to make the decision while running low on funds and feeling overwhelmed. Bad idea. You also don't want to base this decision on marketing plans that don't actually lead to sales. The number of books you print should be based on realistic sales strategies and demand. Period.

The more books you print, the less you will pay per unit. That means that you will make more money per sale if you print more books. However, a large print run isn't the best business decision for every author. Sitting on thousands of books of inventory a year after your launch is pretty much every author's worst nightmare, not to mention the cost of printing and storage costs.

Given that your print quantity should directly reflect the number of books you think you will sell, you might be wondering how you figure this out. We definitely understand that this is not an easy thing to guess. But here are the guiding questions to help you find the right answer:

- Have you presold any copies through either your website or a crowdfunding campaign?

- Do you envision a well-attended launch party? Will people will be incentivized to buy more than one copy of your book?

- Do you have plans to sell your book in bulk, for educational purposes, to corporations or nonprofits, or through your business?

- Do you have an email list of potential buyers with a strategy to engage them before your book is released?

If the answer to most of those questions is yes, consider a larger print run. For a newbie indie author, we'd consider a large print run to be anything above 1,500.

If you answered no to most of the above questions, or if you are simply beside yourself at the thought of guessing how many books you will sell, start small. Printing between 500 and 1,500 copies is a safe place to start and still offers the possibility to earn a profit if you're able to sell a good portion directly.

Before you move on from this chapter, let's dig deeper into the question of how many books you think you can sell in the first year. First, we suggest you take a hard look at your storage options. If budget isn't a large factor, or if you think you will do the vast majority of your sales via Amazon, you might think using a warehouse that fulfills to Amazon is the best option for you.

When printing a large quantity of books, you run the risk of having them sit at a warehouse racking up fees if you don't have a solid strategy in place to build momentum and sell books in the right places at the right time. Without this momentum, you will grow tired of paying storage fees. They add up, especially when inventory isn't moving. The other con of using warehousing and storage services is that you will make less money than if you sell direct.

This is so important it bears repeating: Your focus should be on selling books directly, as this is the way you will make the most money. It is also the most fun—interacting with your readers will be one of the most rewarding experiences of this journey. We recommend that you keep a large portion, maybe even half, of your inventory with you. You'll save on storage costs, be able to track your sales better, and have books at the ready for the spontaneous selling opportunities that arise.

Next, think of your own personal storage options. This also might drive the number of books you print. For example, if you have a huge house or an unused closet in the basement, you have a place to store many boxes of books for free. If you are in a small apartment with no storage, even a few boxes of books might take up too much room.

Aside from storage costs and plans to sell as many books as you can directly, the most important factor to help you select the right number of books to print is your sales goals. Don't stop at an overall or general sales goal. How many books can you sell monthly— through your website, at events, through stores, and via online retailers like Amazon? What are your monthly marketing initiatives to drive sales—speaking gigs, advertising, giveaways and contests, media placements, email marketing campaigns? Large publishers decide how many books to print based on anticipated demand, and in this case, you should follow their lead.

Large publishers also weigh the popularity of competing titles as well as an author's willingness to participate in marketing efforts, fanbase size, publicity plans, and current platform (website traffic, social media fans, booked speaking engagements). Again, you're no different. With your business hat on, plan how to create demand for your book, and then gather the data you need to determine how many books it makes sense to print in your first run. Remember, you will hopefully print more books. Ultimately, the more you think through your marketing plans, the more likely you are to arrive at the right number of books to print.

Per Unit Cost for Printing	
50	
100	
200	
500	
1000	
3000	

Monthly Sales Goals	
1st Quarter	
2nd Quarter	
3rd Quarter	
4th Quarter	

Book Prize

_____ books sold direct at _____ per book = $ _____

_____ books sold via retailers w/_____ % discount = $ _____

Retailer sales goal: _____ per month

Direct sales goal: _____ per month

Goal per quarter:_____

Goal in 1st year:_____

26

What is the best way to sell my book? Amazon? Direct? Some other way?

The short answer to this vital question is that, for most authors, selling direct is the wisest route whenever possible. You will make the most money that way, and as an indie author who has likely put a lot of money into publishing your book, recovering those funds and becoming profitable is important.

However, a direct-only sales model isn't realistic for reaching beyond your immediate networks of followers, friends, family, and colleagues. And with Amazon being queen of book sales, having a presence there is often crucial for visibility. This is the universal author conundrum—the desire to sell books directly to maximize profits, and the understanding that most readers will not venture to author websites to buy books.

So have your book available for sale in the following three ways:

- Directly via your website or live events
- Amazon, as a third-party vendor

- A distribution partner
- Print on demand

Selling Directly via Your Website

While many authors feel overwhelmed at the thought of managing book sales through their websites, services like PayPal make this really simple. A "buy now" button is easy to add to the "Buy My Book" page on your website, and PayPal order submissions will come directly to your email. You can print a packing list and pay for shipping all via PayPal, so it truly is a matter of setting up a PayPal account, having a working printer, and using an envelope/box to ship books. The nice thing about selling books directly (besides making the most money per sale) is that you can have a direct connection to readers this way. You can personally sign books as they are mailed out, add purchasers to your email distribution list, and follow up with readers to ask for a review. You can also host BOGO offers, holiday discounts, and price-matching discounts with Amazon.

In Summary: If you can sell via your website, do. If the idea is too overwhelming to you, then don't!

Amazon, as a Third Party

Selling books on Amazon as a third-party vendor is a cinch once you're set up there. Amazon makes purchasing anything easy, which is why they are a consumer favorite.

Keep in mind that you will make far less money per sale. It is easy to dismiss Amazon and try to distribute yourself as discussed above, but keep in mind that many, many people purchase books on Amazon. Not only that, Amazon's algorithms are powerful marketing tools. People searching for a fantasy book might be directed to your book in Amazon's "people also bought" section on the page, opening you up to a bigger, broader audience.

In Summary: Selling via Amazon as a third party results in less money in your pocket, but it is necessary to sell your book there if you want to reach the biggest possible customer base.

Selling via a Distributor

If you are hoping to sell many copies of your books to organizations such as bookstores, libraries, and corporations, a partnership with a distribution service that can fulfill orders for you will be enormously valuable—if not necessary. While it would be ideal to have these institutions purchase from you directly, often that is not viable for a number of reasons.

The distributor will warehouse your books for a monthly rent and will likely charge a fee for each book they sell. Bookstores sometimes order directly from distributors, but more often they go through a wholesaler as a middleman (Ingram or Baker & Taylor).

When the distributor, wholesaler, and bookseller all take a cut, this also means much less money in your pocket; however, it is an unavoidable expense if you want to diversify your sales channels. Again, this is a business decision. For most authors, having a partnership with a company that helps with distribution means access to more readers. Depending on the service you choose, you will receive monthly statements informing you of how many books were sold during a certain time, minus storage and packing fees. Hopefully, the profits you make from monthly sales will outweigh the fees.

In Summary: Selling via a distributor is an option that you will want to keep open if you are hoping to sell your book to large institutions of any kind.

Print on Demand

A relatively recent addition to the book industry is the ability to print books on demand. Here's how it works: You set up your files with a POD service (IngramSpark and Createspace are the two big ones), and they will print and ship a single copy of your book anytime one is ordered. Booksellers can get your titles through their normal distribution services, and listings will automatically go up on Amazon and other online retailers.

Depending on the exact specifications of your book, POD may or may not be a feasible option. Printing a single copy of your book will be more expensive than printing hundreds, and the service will also take a large percent of your profit. It's not uncommon to only net a couple of dollars on each book sold. If your book is in color or hardcover, it might be impossible to make money on each sale. Plus, the quality of the book will be far lower than what a professional printer would usually produce; the spine may bleed onto the back, colors will be less vivid, and you'll see the occasional smear.

In Summary: Print on demand is a low-investment way to get your book listed for sale, but it can be difficult to turn a profit, and your product will not be particularly impressive.

As we cannot stress enough, getting people to purchase directly from you is key. What are the primary ways you will sell your book direct? Brainstorm here:

My Direct Sales Strategies:

If you decide to sell your book through Amazon or work with a distribution partner to expand your access to traditional sales, what are the primary ways you will optimize your book's presence in those channels? Keep in mind that getting your book listed for sale is the easy part; the hard part is convincing people to buy it! Brainstorm here:

My Traditional Sales Strategies:

27

What are effective ways to promote my book via social media?

Ah, social media. In theory, you would be able to carefully craft and upload a killer Facebook post announcing the launch of your incredible book, and all one thousand of your friends would gleefully (and promptly) buy not one, but two copies each. You'd get to blissfully enjoy the buzz, watch the money roll in, and prepare to write your next bestseller.

If only it were that easy.

With social media, three things make all the difference as to whether a post will fall into obscurity or capture the attention of your peeps and, even more importantly, prompt action. After all, likes, shares, and retweets are gravy; if going viral on social media doesn't translate into sales or more loyal fans, it's time to rethink your strategy.

1. **Create posts that are authentic.** Capture your actual life as an author. Share pics, personal stories, and the real pitfalls of your journey (but don't complain—see chapter

3!). Get vulnerable. Speak to the buyers directly. In some cases those buyers might not be the book audience—children's books authors, for example, are targeting parents and educators, not children.

2. **Create content, not posts. Don't post something for the sake of having something online.** An announcement that your book is available isn't good content. Even a post promoting an offer, special, or gift might not prompt the reaction you want without being paired with thoughtful content. Instead, share resources, ask and answer provocative questions, and inspire your fans. You're an influencer. Create posts, videos, tweets, and articles about the topics your readers find valuable. If you need ideas, repurpose what you've already written—super easy. Joining Facebook groups where your readers hang out is another tip. Another trick: poll your followers on social media with a question like, "What is one question you'd ask your favorite writer over dinner?"

3. **Remember to boost your posts.** Boosting is a cost-effective way of reaching more people.

That all seems pretty straightforward and simple, right? Of course not. We get it; this is all new for some, and quite a challenge for most.

Over the years, we have seen our fair share of frustrated authors give up on social media after months of fruitless interactions, wasted time, and very few results. "It's like screaming into the wind!" one author recently said. We understand. For every author who has found luck with a social media post that has gone viral, there are fifty more who just aren't moving books that way.

Before you begin any social media campaign, ask yourself the following questions:

- **Which platform will work best?** Be thoughtful about this answer. The platform you are most comfortable using might not be the best way to reach your readers and buyers.

- **How am I going to ensure my target buyers are going to receive the message?** Again, think this through. Can you send the post to certain people via email or a direct message on Facebook? (We never recommend tagging people in posts.) Can you utilize a popular hashtag to get in front of a new audience? Can you create an offer so enticing that it will catch the eye of key people?

- **How's my timing?** If you have a perfect holiday gift book, offering a BOGO deal on your website makes perfect sense at the beginning of December. If your book is poetry, can you time your offer for National Poetry Month in April or the birthday of your favorite poet?

- **How willing am I to promote this offer?** You should be prepared to see your social media campaign through. That means cross-posting, or making sure your posts are available on multiple social media platforms, thanking people for their purchases, and strategically boosting posts.

- **Can I create a partnership which might help my post?** How can you creatively share your offer with the wider community? Can you partner with an artist for a unique illustration? Can you donate a certain percentage of your sales to a cause that is relevant to your book/brand? Can you ask a key endorser to help you spread the word?

Next, create the social media post. Text is usually not enough. How can you use graphics to enhance your message? Visit wiseink.com/resources for some examples of social media posts done right!

Finally, in the world of social media, where people are inundated every single day with images, ads, offers, and gimmicks, even your best efforts might go unnoticed. That's okay. If you find yourself getting frustrated, take a break. Do a little research using your book's keywords to get a sense of the content already out there. A couple of years ago, we accidentally discovered that book bloggers and other publishers were posting the most beautiful photos of books on Instagram. They were using cool props, integrating color and nature, and putting a lot more effort into capturing the essence of the story. Our photos were pretty bland by comparison. Without taking a step back and doing some online ~~stalking~~ research, we would have continued to thoughtlessly post photos of our favorite books without realizing that it was far past time to up our ante if we wanted to get noticed.

Even though we've come a long way, we're still not perfect by a long shot. But we know that storytelling and showing our followers who we truly are and why they matter to us is key.

Moral of the story: find a way to connect with your audience directly and with intention. A little work on the front end pays off. Whether you're blogging, sending crafted content to your email list, or attending an event, find your voice, and have fun speaking to your followers as you would to a friend over coffee.

Brainstorm ideas here for social media posts that might generate sales. Examples include rhetorical questions having to do with your book/brand [ex. 'Who are some of your writing heroes?' or 'What are some of your tips for staying within a budget?'], books that have inspired you, organizations doing important work related to your book/brand, and extra material from your book that might have been left on the cutting room floor. Everything is fair game! Use social media to tell your story and endear people to YOU.

My Post Ideas to Generate Sales:

_____

_____

_____

_____

28

What are some cheap and easy ways to market my book?

This is a question we wish more authors asked. Cheap and easy marketing is often the most effective marketing. In fact, it's likely that your most lucrative marketing efforts will come at zero cost. Don't assume that spending thousands of dollars with a PR agency is a requirement to reach your sales goals. It's not. In fact, many authors who have invested in hiring expensive PR services end up doing far better on their own.

On the flip side, cheap and easy marketing is often time-consuming. If you have more than twenty hours a week to market your book, you are one lucky author. And you're a perfect candidate for a DIY marketing strategy. If you are like most authors we work with, you are juggling family obligations, a job or two, and a hectic schedule, so carving out time to market your book will be challenging and you will likely need help. With or without help, most authors spend most of their marketing time doing a combination of the following:

- Research
- Outreach
- Follow-up
- Networking
- Content creation

What's nice about those marketing tactics is that there is a plethora of ways to go about doing them cheaply. You can do market research at the library for free and access tons of free knowledge online; you can find contact info for media contacts on your own; you can do your own follow-up; you can find plenty of free networking opportunities; and you can write your own content. But the hard truth is that you will need to choose carefully where it makes the most sense to spend your time.

Ultimately, the cheapest and easiest way to market your book is to tell people about it. End of story. If you can afford to do nothing else, tell five strangers about your book every day for the first year. And then ask for free help. Friends organically promoting your book on your behalf will prove to be better than almost any paid marketing service you might solicit. Here's a list of other cheap and easy ways to market your book (101 Wise Marketing Ideas can be found on page 184):

- **Create a "website-only deal."** Buy-one-get-one-free, buy one at half the cover price, buy one and shipping is free—the options are endless. Make a dynamic graphic, post it on social media, and boost the post. Easy.

- **Utilize your email list and engage your fans.** Send out an email blast asking people to take a picture of themselves holding your book in an obscure place. Ask your list to review your book on Amazon and Goodreads. Thank them for purchasing your book and ask them to gift a copy to someone in their network who might be a perfect connection for you.

- **Write an article.** Maybe it's about the writing process, maybe it's an "additional" chapter to your book, maybe it's some sort of Q&A. Pitch that to *HuffPost*, *Buzzfeed*, or any other blog with a large following.

- **Host a giveaway on Goodreads.** They are simple to do, and a great way to get people to add your book to their "to-read" bookshelves. (Note: as of January 2018, there is a fee involved for hosting a giveaway on Goodreads.)

- **Social Media.** If you've tapped out your resources on LinkedIn, try Facebook. If you have never been a part of a book discussion on Twitter, try that.

- **Foster a win-win partnership.** Maybe with your local school's book fair, maybe with an artist who can create a complimentary piece of work for your book, maybe with a nonprofit you can help raise funds for. Remember, you are doing more than just selling books, you are selling your brand, vision, and message.

Think outside the box and beyond your book. Brainstorm here the things you haven't tried yet, but might want to give a chance:

Outside the Box Sales Strategies:

How do I get my book into libraries?

Getting your book into libraries (some of our favorite places in the world) should be a goal for most authors. If we had a magical formula for getting all 100,000-plus libraries in the United States to buy five copies of every book, we would gladly share it with you. Alas, if you haven't figured it out yet, there is no magic bullet for selling your book.

But here are the four things that help get your book into libraries, if that is your goal:

1. **Distribution.** Make sure your book is available via standard distribution (Ingram, Baker & Taylor, etc). Similar to bookstores, libraries will rarely purchase books directly from you or your website.

2. **Relationship.** That could mean going into your local branch and introducing yourself, or maybe offering a class to teach or a book talk to give. Ask them how they order books and familiarize yourself with their processes.

3. **Visibility.** Get yourself featured in publications that wind up in the hands of librarians. For example, the ALA (American Library Association) has a list of publications

that they are associated with; try to get yourself a featured article or even an ad in one of those publications.

4. **Reviews.** Spring for an editorial review from a reputable source such as *Kirkus* or *Clarion*. Librarians often read *Kirkus* to see what the new, great titles are.

Use this chart to track your correspondence with local libraries:

Libraries to contact and library associations to pitch	Ideas for pitches and progress

30

How do I reach book clubs?

Book clubs are powerful. With origins in eighteenth-century Paris salons and Victorian parlors, book clubs have long been in the public consciousness. Today, a large number of avid readers depend on book clubs to discover new authors and participate in provocative group discussions. A book club is, for many readers, the primary way to choose which books they're going to read. In the past, an "Oprah's Book Club" sticker placed on a cover pretty much guaranteed a work's *NYT* bestseller status. Now, plenty of celebrities recommend books; Reese Witherspoon, for example, has an online book club that you can follow using the hashtag #RWBookClub. Library-hosted book clubs are more popular than ever thanks to ebook loan services like Overdrive and Hoopla. And thanks to social media, book clubs can talk to each other and their featured authors. Book clubs are shaking things up. They're also evolving, no longer only in-person. By prompting a group of people to all buy the same book, read it together, and then talk about it, book clubs make the solitary act of reading a social event.

So what does all this mean for your book? First, you need to factor how your book could thrive in an experience where many people are consuming it together. Next, ask yourself,

How can I make it easy for book clubs to find my book? and *What tools can I create to help book clubs discuss it?*

Reaching book clubs is not about pounding the pavement to get them interested in your book. Of course, in your immediate network are probably a few willing people able to suggest or select your book for their book clubs. Absolutely pursue those opportunities. Ask your fans to recommend your book to their book clubs and then make yourself available to participate in the discussion. However, reaching hundreds of book clubs through outreach will take a lot of time and effort, and again, we're marketing wisely.

So we want you to devise a particular plan, factoring in the strategies of larger book publishers for leveraging book clubs. After all, it's no secret that a book recommendation borne out of a book club carries more weight than a regular recommendation. Groups of people don't spend hours every month talking about a boring, badly written book, right?

Here are a few tried and true ways of making your book appeal to the book club crowd:

- **Offer a deal.** Discount your book for bulk book-club orders. If your book retails for $15.99, offer ten books for $100.

- **Add a bonus.** Offer, on top of a discount, a thirty-minute Skype or in-person Q&A for the book club. It'll give them something extra to break up the monotony of the usual discussion everyone is used to.

- **Write your own discussion questions.** Many authors ignore this simple tool for helping their readers engage with the books at the next level. Put thoughtfully crafted questions in the back of your book, or in an easily downloadable PDF on your website or Facebook page. When writing these questions, focus on themes and character development rather than plot.

- **Include extra content.** Have a scene that was left on the cutting-room floor? What about a related short story? Other ideas include an alternate ending, a video of you discussing your favorite or most emotional aspect of your book, a family tree of your characters, a map of the places in the book, or content written from the perspective of a character from the book.

- **Optimize your book's ability to be curated on "Best Books" lists.** On Pinterest, on websites like Bustle and Buzzfeed, and in magazines, you've likely seen the "Best Books of This Year" or "What to Read After [big blockbuster book]" lists. Curate your own lists—with your book included on them—and then promote them online. Do a bit of research and suggest your book to outlets where those lists might be created—bloggers and online book reviewers are a good place to start. You only need to get on one of those lists. Once you have, promote it everywhere—marketing materials, social media accounts, even your email signature.

- **Create a book club kit.** Make it easy for book clubs. Create an online destination on your website where they can access a coupon code for buying directly from you, a downloadable reading guide PDF, and bonuses or freebies created specifically for them.

31

What is a blog tour, and should I do one?

Blog tours are the "virtual" version of a book tour. Instead of hopping on a plane and visiting places all over the country to promote your book (something that's likely to decimate your marketing budget), you can instead send copies of your book to book bloggers, who will in turn review your book on their blogs. Blog tours are often timed to happen in conjunction with the release of your book, to generate some buzz around your title. Online buzz is almost always a good thing!

There are people—lots of people—who coordinate blog tours as their full-time jobs. Let that sink in for a second. Their entire work week is dedicated to securing blog tour stops, working on the timing of those stops, and ensuring posts are published. We tell you that so you are 100 percent aware that while securing a blog tour doesn't seem like hard work, it most certainly is time-consuming. Blog tour coordinators often have relationships with the bloggers they work with, compensate them for timely posts, and are constantly researching new bloggers to partner with.

Let's break down the pros and cons of securing a blog tour:

Pros	Cons
• A blog tour is a wonderful way to tap into readers and bloggers interested in your genre all over the world.	• Blog tours can be expensive, depending on how many "stops" you secure and how reputable the blog tour operator is.
• Each and every blog tour stop can be used as a way of connecting to a new audience. You can comment on posts, participate in a Q&A, host a giveaway, and use positive feedback for your own social media and marketing purposes.	• Blog tours often do not immediately translate into sales. This is important, so we will repeat it. **Blog tours do not always translate into sales.** Blog tours are effective to help you create buzz, reviews, and content for your own purposes, all of which are definitely valuable but will probably not move a ton of inventory.
• Hiring someone to coordinate a blog tour for you frees up a lot of free time for you to work on different marketing strategies.	• It is possible that you will receive negative reviews.

You should consider a blog tour if:

- **You write fiction, especially YA, romance, or fantasy.** Fiction books tend to get much more online buzz from bloggers than nonfiction.

- **You are just beginning to build your platform and are looking to extend your reach in any way possible.** A blog tour can help you tap into communities you didn't know existed. And if relationship-building with bloggers is a good strategy for your book, then a blog tour is a good way to do that.

- **You have a hard time finding content for social media.** Having an active blog tour will give you lots of unique ways to engage on social media.

- **You have limited time to devote to getting your book out into the world.** Again, coordinating blog tours is complicated, and if you don't have the time to do it then hiring someone to help you makes sense.

You might want to skip the blog tour if:

- **You write nonfiction or very specific genre fiction.** If your audience is extremely specific, chances are having your book on a blogger's broad review site won't be beneficial.

- **You already have a large platform.** Can you ask the people already following or subscribed to your list to read, review, and post about your book? If so, you've already done more than half the work of a blog tour coordinator.

- **You are unable or unwilling to promote the blog stops on social media.** As with any marketing effort, the results will depend largely on your willingness to promote them. If you aren't on any social media sites and won't promote the tour stops, then your posts will likely not generate much buzz.

- **You're out of marketing funds.** Hiring someone to run a blog tour can be expensive, and you often won't see an immediate sales bump. If you're considering a blog tour, it is crucial that you understand this. You certainly *can* do the work of a blog tour coordinator yourself by reaching out to bloggers you think would be perfect reviewers. Or you can skip this marketing strategy altogether, instead focusing on something that you think will better help you meet your sales goals.

32

I want to schedule book signings and events at bookstores. How do I create a successful bookstore event?

First of all, we want to state for the record that we love bookstores. Most authors do. That's why, when they envision becoming a successful author, part of that picture includes having a bookstore event. What says *I've arrived* better than a packed bookstore to support the release and promotion of your book?

What we write in the following section might imply that we don't think bookstore signings are a good idea—that is not the case. What we do think is that bookstore signings should be thought out strategically.

To put this in context, when Dara's first book, *The Indie Author Revolution,* was published a few years ago, the first thing she did was plan her launch event. We were excited—a book written especially for the indie author community, outlining all the steps to publish with or without a team! Even though we had most often worked with authors to plan their book events at homes, restaurants, community centers, and arts spaces, we thought we'd partner with a popular indie bookstore in downtown Minneapolis for the *Indie Author Revolution* launch event. We loved the store, had a personal relationship with the events manager, and knew we could draw a crowd. On the day of the event, we packed the back of the store with more than seventy-five people, worked with a caterer (Dara's husband happens to own a restaurant), and executed what we thought had been a decent launch party. We'd even promoted the event in our local newspaper, which unexpectedly resulted in a few—not many, but a few—extra attendees from our local community. Dara's family and our friends all came out, and several bought multiple copies.

At the end of the evening, we couldn't wait to talk to the bookstore staff to hear their estimate of how many books were sold. "We think we sold about one hundred copies," said one of the staff, fairly nonchalantly. Our friend and events manager for the store congratulated us on a successful night as we were packing up, but not without adding, "I just wish we could've gotten more people in." *Ouch*, we thought. At the time, his comment stung quite a bit. Now, looking back, it makes sense why he said that—and also why we chose not to organize a launch event for *this* book at a bookstore.

If you are an indie author who already has a huge fanbase, you are at an advantage in many ways. Signings are one of them. When you already have a group of fans dying for the chance to meet you in person and receive a signed book, bookstore signings are a wonderful way to engage an audience who knows you and is familiar with the content you write. Bookstores prefer this kind of author because they're likely to draw in more foot traffic, fill the store, and drive sales of other books.

If you are an indie author who is only beginning to build a fanbase, bookstore events are trickier. Think about it—how often do you make plans to visit an unknown author to get a signed copy of their book? We're guessing rarely, if ever. Also factor in the time of day of a signing and how much foot traffic the bookstore gets during that time, and bookstore signings can be lonely events indeed.

The other challenges are purely financial. It's no secret that bookstores are not making the money they used to, thanks to Amazon and the infinite free content of the internet. People don't buy as many books in bookstores anymore. Additionally, when you sign books at a bookstore, they will likely charge full price for your book. Most bookstores will then take a percentage of each sale, usually 40–50 percent. This is a lose-lose for you. With the *Indie Author Revolution,* one hundred sold books would have translated into about $1,595 in sales if the books had been sold direct and at full price, at a nonretail venue like a restaurant. Because of the discount, almost half of that went to the bookstore. Also, depending on the store, an event selling fewer than a hundred copies is not considered a home run, especially factoring in their time to coordinate the event and the sacrifice of precious store space to accomodate you and those who might support you.

These reasons are why we suggest that before reaching out to your local bookstore to schedule signings for your book, you should consider the following:

- Bookstores are in the business of making sales, and the way they do that is by bringing people into the store. How are you going to help bring a crowd into the store that day?

- How can you engage an audience there? Can you give a talk, do a demonstration, or have some sort of Q&A session? It is not going to be enough to read your work—how will you make people feel like you are providing them with something more?

- How can you increase your odds of having the signing be financially lucrative for you? If your book is geared toward fathers, can you schedule a book signing around Father's Day? Can you ask the bookstore when the most foot traffic tends to take place and schedule your signing at that time?

The good news is that bookstores, even large Barnes & Noble chains, often welcome authors in for signings. Scheduling a signing can be as simple as going into the bookstore or sending an email with your sell sheet, a complimentary copy of your book, and your thoughts about how hosting a signing with you would be a win-win.

As with all things indie publishing, we highly recommend starting with your local community and working out from there. Use the space below to list your local bookstores, the event contact person, and the date you reached out.

Bookstore	Event Contact Person	Date I Reached Out

Lastly, be sure to take photos at your event and spread the word via social media.

How do I woo booksellers and retailers in general?

When you approach bookstores, and retailers in general, about carrying your title, you will likely have a variety of experiences depending on the size of the stores, their locations, and their experiences working with authors. It can be all over the place. Do a bit of legwork ahead of time to determine where your book would thrive on the shelf. In the immediate five-mile radius around where you live, some stores will be better able to support your book than others.

Although just getting your book on the shelves can be enough of a challenge, the real goal is to get booksellers to recommend your book. If your novel goes straight on the shelf, it will quite possibly sit there undisturbed for six months before getting returned. If your book has a "staff pick" bookmark or is featured on a display, it can be up to ten times more likely to sell!

Unlike a large, traditional publisher, you don't have a sales rep privy to the data about which stores are best for your book. So here are a few things to do before reaching out to booksellers and retailers:

1. **Learn how they operate.** Is there an events coordinator you should talk to about a signing or reading? How do they buy books? Which books are displayed most prominently in their store? Who are the authors they feature and have events for the most—national bestsellers, local authors, or a combination?

2. **Know exactly where your book belongs.** The more you can help a bookstore out, the better. Get familiar with where your book fits in a store so that when you pitch, you know exactly what niche you're offering to fill.

When you are approaching booksellers or retailers about carrying your book, here are a few dos and don'ts to keep in mind:

Do	Don't
• Be extraordinarily respectful of their time. Address them as Mr. or Ms. in the email, and thank them for consideration. Try to find out who is in charge of book ordering and reach out to them directly; most bookstore employees have little say over which books the store carries.	• Forget to proofread your emails before they go out. Make sure you are addressing people correctly and your correspondence with them is free from typos or grammatical errors.
• Give them a complimentary copy of your book or a sell sheet (printed in color on nice paper) so they can get a sense of the quality of your book. Consider including some display ideas ("Books to Read by the Fire" or "Fantasy Books by Women," etc.) featuring your book and others the bookseller might have in stock.	• Just send them a link to your book on Amazon. The market is saturated with books of varying qualities, and they will not want to carry your book without knowing it's of high quality.
• Be willing to accommodate whatever works best for their business model, be it consignment, purchasing in bulk from you directly, or purchasing from a distributor.	• Be inflexible about purchasing or create unnecessary hassle on their end.
• Offer to bring people into their store. Host a class, do a talk, do a signing, and promote them on your social media.	• Assume that just because your book is on the shelf the store will promote it. That work is still yours!

What are "outside the box" ideas for marketing my book?

We have found that the authors who are most successful at book sales are willing to try different ways of connecting with readers. However, connecting with readers is different for everyone—each genre, author, and message is unique. Here is a list of a few ways to stretch yourself outside the "normal" marketing channels to reach a new audience:

- Contact a small business relevant to your content and offer them a discount on a bulk order of your book for their promotional purposes. The pitch could look something like this:

  Dear [owner] (find out their name and email, and make this a personal greeting),

  I have been a frequent customer of yours for years, and have always loved patronizing your store. I recently saw that you are running a special promotion for the holidays, and I have a holiday gift book I think would make a wonderful "gift with purchase." My book retails for $19.99, but I would be happy to extend you a 50 percent discount on an order of 25 or more books. I would also be happy to promote the sale on my social *media sites and hopefully draw in a wonderful holiday crowd for your store. Looking forward to hearing your thoughts on how we can partner together!*

Notice how this simple email clearly states the connection to the business, the offer, and the fact that you would be partnering with them to create a win-win situation.

- Contact a small business relevant to your book and ask if you can help promote them in some way in exchange for placement in their store. For example:

    Dear [owner],

    I have been a customer at your bake shop for many years, and while I know you normally only sell baking items in your store, I think my book about a cooking school mystery would be a wonderful addition to your shop. With Valentine's Day coming in a month, would you consider selling my books on consignment there? I was thinking we could put a coupon or custom bookmark advertising your business inside the book, so anyone who purchases the book will come back for more of your baked goods. Looking forward to hearing from you!

    Again, notice that this is phrased in a way that makes it a win-win situation.

- Host an event. If you haven't figured it out already, we love events. Events are a great way to bring people to you and engage your readers. We highly recommend having a certain number of books be a part of your speaking fee. You can host something in your home, at someone else's book club, at a library, at a community center, or anywhere else you have connections.

- Contact a small business and ask if you could provide a coupon for your book (or some sort of fun freebie, like a bookmark) as something they include with all the receipts they give to customers during a given time. Just as in the examples above, you will need to present this in a way that is a win-win for both of you.

- Do some digging into associations that might be interested in purchasing your book in bulk. A search on the Directory of Associations website will yield thousands of possibilities. Can you contact the directors there and ask to be a speaker, or perhaps advertise or sell your book at their next event?

- Take part in a reading. It can be an open mic night, a community event, or a panel discussion. Contact members of the local arts scene who might be able to host you.

- Find social media personalities who might be interested in reviewing your book and contact them to offer a free copy. Think beyond just Facebook—look at YouTube, Twitter, and even Snapchat.

- Connect with readers in a new way. There are wonderful reading forums on Reddit, Pinterest, and Goodreads, to name just a few.

- Subscription/gift boxes are getting more popular every day. Can you find a subscription box company to contact and partner with? Similar to pitching yourself to any business, you will want to extend a bulk order discount and explain how a partnership with you could be a win-win.

- Create new graphics for your book. You can create graphics that show images of your book launch, positive reviews you've received, or even inspirational quotes tangentially related to your subject matter.

- Guest post on a blog. We can't overstate the importance of using content to sell your book. Create a blog post about a theme in your book or something that will capture your audience's attention. Pitch your post to blogs that have large followings!

Organize your "out of the box" thoughts below:

> **Possible events I could host:**
>
> _____
>
> _____
>
> _____
>
> _____

Small businesses or associations I could partner with:

_____

_____

_____

_____

_____

_____

Subscription/gift box companies that might be interested in featuring my book:

_____

_____

_____

_____

_____

_____

Blogs I would like to be featured on, as well as content ideas:

_____

_____

_____

_____

_____

_____

Other "out of the box" ideas!

_____

_____

_____

_____

_____

35

How do I pitch my book to organizations like schools, businesses, and nonprofits?

First of all, kudos for thinking along these lines. Bulk sales to large organizations are the secret of authors who earn a considerable income selling books. Organizations often have the budgets and resources to make large purchases, and if you find the right organization, your sales potential is near limitless. Over the years, we've witnessed authors across genres sell thousands of books to corporations, charities, membership organizations, local governments, and schools. For many of them, it took time to find the appropriate contact person and then persistent follow-up to clinch the deal. Just before this book went to press, we learned that a Wise Ink author received an order from a nationally known training organization for five thousand copies of his book. This is likely just the first of many bulk orders for this particular author, who thoughtfully devised a strategy that included creating training programs and workshops to accompany his book.

Before you start sending out emails to organizations you think would buy your book in bulk, it is important to ask yourself the following questions:

- **Is this the right organization?** It's easy to get caught up in the idea of having a school district purchase your novel to use in their curriculum or a corporation purchase your business book to give to new hires, but the last thing you want to do is create a generic pitch and hope someone picks it up. The "right" organization for you is going to have concrete ties to your book and message. They are going to be an organization you have thoroughly researched, and you'll need to have a real understanding of their values and goals and how they relate to yours. They should also be an organization that you feel can benefit you beyond your book, via speaking engagements or supplemental materials.

- **What are my personal connections to this organization?** As with many things in life, a lot is "who you know." If you have a personal connection, use it! But again, be strategic and respectful. Some people will be happy to give you the name and email address of their company's CEO, while others might not for any number of reasons. When using a personal connection of any kind, be honest with your inquiry, ask them if they are willing to help, and thank them profusely for making the connections for you. If the connections don't pan out, they don't pan out. Don't ever make anyone else feel obligated to do your marketing work!

- **Who is the right person or group to contact?** It may seem that sending an email to a school principal is the most logical way to get straight to the decision-maker at the school, but that is not necessarily the case. The librarian or media specialist might be the right person to contact instead. Or, if you are hoping to be a part of the school book fair, the Parent-Teacher Association might be your best contact. Similarly, the CEO of the company often won't have the time or willingness to look over your request, but the person in charge of event planning might. Never expect anything to come from a blank "To Whom It May Concern" email—this is the perfect way to have your mail marked as spam. Take the time to figure out who the decision-maker is for your purposes, and contact them singularly and directly.

- **Is my offer irresistible?** First, make sure your letter or email doesn't have typos or grammatical errors. Also, make it good. Don't be vague, generic, or—worst of all—boring. Take the time to create a thoughtful, articulate, and personal note. Show an organization that you've done your homework, you understand what is important to them, and you bring something to the table that they will find valuable. Your letter is about *them*, not about you. This is the time to highlight the benefits of your book and why those benefits serve the organization. Share the success stories and testimonials of other organizations. If your book doesn't have an organic tie-in with what the organization is about but you have a presentation or workshop that could get you in the door, pitch that instead. You'll still likely be able to sell books.

Here are general pitching dos and don'ts to help you:

Do	Don't
• Find the right organization for you, and show that you know who they are and what they stand for.	• Send out a blast pitch copying every CEO in your industry. This will get you nowhere.
• Send either an email or a letter. If you send an email, attach the first chapter of your book as a sample, or offer to send them an ARC or finished copy of your book. If you send a letter, include a copy.	• Send nonstop follow-up. If you send out a pitch, feel free to follow up two to four weeks later if you haven't heard anything. If after a follow-up you still don't hear back, you can likely consider that possibility closed (for now).
• Describe how a partnership with you is a win-win. Make sure to specify what "extras" you will provide with purchase. Make it something enticing for them and their stakeholders.	• Put any personal contacts you have into an awkward position. Be extraordinarily respectful of people's business connections and relationships.
• Create a pitch that is memorable. Can you add any swag you have to your mailer? Can you insert your sense of humor, if that is appropriate?	• Go overboard. Sending a box with your book, flowers, candy, glitter, and candles is unnecessary.
	• Give up. There are literally thousands of places you can pitch your book to. Take it one pitch at a time, and keep trying.

Brainstorm potential partnerships with large organizations:

Organization	Key Contact/ Personal Connection	Pitch Ideas

Should I submit my book for awards?

It might seem this question should have a simple, yes-or-no answer. We know, we've said "it depends" quite a bit, but hang in there with us on this one. Awards are one of the few low-hanging-fruit action items that are easy for most authors to justify. One author we worked with submitted his book for more than sixty awards! He created the most impressive spreadsheet we've ever seen and spent hours compiling a list of awards to submit his book to. Of course, he won a bunch of them, and he enjoyed the acclaim that came with saying he was an "award-winning author." It does have a nice ring to it, after all. But before you go down the road of entering awards, it's important to understand a few things:

- **Not all awards are created equal.** Just like an Academy Award is more high-profile than an award from your local community theater, the same goes for book awards, particularly indie book awards. Be careful before entering an award competition that you are participating in a reputable contest.

- **Fees.** Entering your book for an award competition almost always includes paying a fee. This is okay and expected. Judges read many, many manuscripts, and subsequently work to announce and sometimes promote the winning titles on their website, so it is logical to expect a submission fee. Usually, the fee per title, per genre, is around fifty to one hundred dollars.

- **No guarantee.** There are almost no awards that will catapult your book into *New York Times* bestseller status. If this is your expectation, you are bound to be disappointed.

- **Requires promotion.** Winning an award is only as valuable as you make it. This means that if you win an award, you can't just hope your local paper contacts you about it—*you* need to contact them with an updated press release.

Before even considering entering an award contest, revisit the goals you brainstormed in the first chapter. If winning an award will help you meet those goals, then you might want to consider entering. If not, then don't. It's really as simple as that.

Instances where an award win might be a good boost for you include:

- You are hoping to break into the literary world and show you have writing chops.

- You do a lot of trade shows and events, and having an award sticker on the cover of your book might attract potential readers.

- You are hoping to catch the attention of a decision-maker who might be swayed by an award win, such as a school or business looking for curriculum materials.

- You have a strategy to leverage award wins to promote your brand as a whole, whether on social media, in your industry and community, or both.

Instances where an award win might not be all that beneficial:

- You already have a large network and are highly involved in your brand and messaging. An award win isn't going to expand your fanbase, per se.

- You already have contacts and contracts with key decision-makers, and an award win isn't something that will make or break those deals.

- You're unlikely to use the win as a way of promoting your brand as a whole, whether on social media, in the community, or both.

- You don't plan on reprinting your book in the future with the image of the award seal added to your front cover.

With these things in mind, brainstorm ways an award win might be beneficial for you. Be specific.

If I win awards, my promotion plans include:

If you struggled to come up with anything to put in the box above, consider putting plans for awards submissions on the back burner for now. Awards are expensive to enter and can be time-consuming.

If you have several bullet points listed, you are a good candidate for an award. Here are a few things to keep in mind as you research award opportunities that are the right fit:

- Do not enter any and every award you find in a Google search. We can't stress this enough. Choose reputable awards, and consider reaching out to past award winners for insight into their experience and how the award served their marketing efforts.

- Carefully select your categories. If you can't find the right category for your book, then consider the award not a good fit for your book.

- Set an award budget and stick to it. Submission fees add up, and it's easy to get carried away and spend a lot of money on those award entries. Your award budget should be part of your overall marketing budget.

Here are a few of our favorite award opportunities:

- The IBPA Ben Franklin Awards
- The Writer's Digest Self-Published Book Awards
- The IPPY Awards
- Any regional book awards in your state or community

Now take some time and research awards that you might enter your book into. Keep track of your award submissions here:

Award Name/ Website	Submission Deadline	Fee	Progress/ Notes

If you win an award, you will want to be sure to spread the good word! Send an email out to your email list, create a social media graphic to post, and draft a press release to give to media outlets to see if they'd be willing to do a story on you and your book.

Do I *really* need to be a public speaker?

The short answer is *probably*. When we started out, we were novice speakers. We sheepishly admit to having sweaty palms while giving the most boring presentations about publishing. We learned the hard way that no one wants to sit for ninety minutes learning about editing and the pitfalls of book production. Yikes!

But as we've gotten better and better at presenting our ideas to the public, we've come to see just how valuable a good speech can be. Over the years, we've come to see that public speaking has opened doors not only for us but also for our authors. We often speak more than fifteen times a year as panelists, keynote speakers, and facilitators of workshops.

If you're still not convinced that speaking is for you, let's step back for a second and reflect on the nature of book publishing today. We live in an age of saturation. Between apps, social media, games, and streaming, every author's book is competing against many other things vying for the attention of busy readers with a limited number of hours per day. Your book, no matter how unique and special, is one of roughly one million books published each and every year. Simply put, unless you get an immeasurably lucky break, you're going to have to put yourself in front of your audience again and again. Speaking, in our opinion, is an effective way to do that.

If you're having heart palpitations right now, we have good news. Speaking does not need to be uncomfortable. You are in charge of where you decide to speak, and there are all kinds of ways to talk to an audience. Sure, there's traditional speaking in front of a large crowd, but speaking for you might consist of poetry readings and open mic nights or online videos and courses. Think of speaking as a way to be visible to your audience in a way that promotes your content and increases your credibility. You can be nontraditional with it. Engaging with your audience this way is not only rewarding but also lucrative. Most of our authors who speak regularly—at conferences, organizations, and events—sell significant quantities of their books at one time. Moreover, if they have other products or services beyond their books, speaking helps sell those too.

Many books lend themselves to several natural presentations, workshops, and courses. If you have a nonfiction book about how to run a company, your content easily lends itself to speaking about your strategies. If you have a cookbook, your speaking events are perfectly suited to cooking demos. If you have a children's book, your speaking events might be Q&A sessions at schools or demonstrations along with your illustrator.

We have found that fiction writers, especially writers who don't have formal writing training or a background in teaching, struggle the most with creating marketable speaking presentations. If you are an accountant by day and a sci-fi writer at night, finding a topic to speak about might prove challenging. You might wonder what topics traditional corporations would hire you to come in and talk about, although storytelling techniques are an incredibly popular topic in business spaces right now. The key to discovering what you should talk about is to create a list of the following:

1. Topics you enjoy talking or teaching others about

2. Topics you have spent the most time and money learning about

3. Stories in your life that will inspire others to action

4. Lessons and mistakes that changed your life and that others can learn from

5. Shortcuts and processes you either created or know well that will save others time, money, or embarrassment

No matter where you are on the spectrum, use the space below to brainstorm topics you would feel comfortable speaking about as they pertain to your book. Think beyond the subject matter if that is appropriate. Can you speak about the writing process? Craft? Tips and tricks you've learned on your way?

Topics or Presentations that compliment my book include:

_____

_____

_____

_____

_____

_____

_____

If your box is empty, or close to empty, here are a few more tips for getting your feet wet in the speaking world:

•   Watch other speakers in your genre. We cannot stress this enough. Check out a myriad of presentations online and in your community and see how other writers in your genre engage their audience through speaking.

- Become aware of the literary events in your community and join them.

- Connect with people who might be able to help you. Maybe you can partner with another writer, or illustrator, or someone else who can complement your book.

And finally, here are a few of our favorite resources to help bolster your speaking ambitions.

- **Craig Valentine's book** *World Class Speaking*: Craig's book is one we recommend to authors who want a specific formula to craft an engaging and effective presentation.

- **Toastmasters International:** One of the best organizations you can join to develop your speaking skills. You'll also have an instant network of supportive thought leaders and experts.

- **TED Talks:** If you want to see examples of powerful presentations that captivate audiences, TED Talks are the perfect resource. TED Talk speakers are coached for weeks before presenting on their topic, and each speaker is hand-selected.

- **Ignite:** Ignite events are held around the country and are dynamic places to attend. Each speaker gets five minutes and twenty slides to present on their topic. The speakers and presentations are as diverse as you can imagine, which always makes for a riveting and enlightening experience.

38

How much should I charge for my speaking events?

It will vary, and this is a good thing. Being flexible and having a range will lead to more opportunities. Your speaking fee will often depend on your time, expertise, and offer, and the ability of the host to pay. But speaking for free can often lead to accomplishing your bigger-picture goals.

We don't recommend telling the world that you don't have a fee. But we also don't recommend turning down any opportunity that doesn't pay. One author has a fee of between $150 and $2,000 depending on the budget of the organization hiring him. He has a series of children's books and has successfully marketed himself to libraries across his state. He has a program for children and families that includes an educational component. The counties that hire him cover his travel, give him an honorarium, and purchase a bulk order of books.

Use the chart on the following page to help guide your decision about how much to charge.

Question:	Answer:
About how much is a person of my expertise paid per hour for their knowledge? (For example, if you are a life coach just starting out, your hourly fee might be $60. If you are a chef with a cookbook who earns approximately $200 per hour for catering/cooking, note that. If you are a fiction author who has never spoken about your craft before, you might be closer to $20 or $30 per hour. Be careful not to over- or undersell what your time is worth.)	
About how much time will I devote to each particular speaking event? (All day? Half a day? One hour? Fifteen minutes of Q&A? Note that you might have several different types of speaking events, so you might have multiple answers to this question.)	
About how much will I spend on materials for my event? (Include photocopies and handouts, and definitely include copies of your book!)	
How labor-intensive will my speaking event be? (For example, a panel discussion with other authors will involve little to no preparation; however, a cooking demo or a week-long workshop involving lesson plans would take many hours to prepare. Rate each event as small, medium, or large in terms of preparation and labor.)	
What is the ability of my host to pay me for my speaking event? (If you are speaking to multinational corporations, chances are there is a large pool of money dedicated to hosting speakers like you. If you are speaking to nonprofits or public schools, paying you for your time might be more difficult. Make a list of potential hosts and what you think they might be able to pay you for speaking.)	
What is my willingness to travel? (It is customary for the host to pay for your travel, and you will want to be very careful to be respectful of their funds. Often, speakers include travel expenses that don't involve an airplane, hotel, and rental car in their general speaking fee. If you are being hosted by someone flying you out to them, those travel fees should be considered separately.)	

You'll see that your answers will not add up easily, meaning that your speaking fee will not always be consistent. That is okay. Here is our suggestion for broaching the speaking fee subject with your potential event hosts:

Dear [Potential Host],

Thank you so much for your consideration in hosting me to speak at your facility! I am looking forward to this wonderful opportunity.

My typical fee for a two-hour presentation is $250, which includes 10 copies of my book for you to keep and distribute as you like. I would certainly appreciate the ability to sell books after my speaking event as well. However, I am careful to customize each of my speaking events to be sure I am giving each organization what is most valuable to them. Please let me know if this fee works for you, or if there is any other agreement we can come to together.

Thanks again,
[Wonderful Author]

Here are a few final tips for your speaking events:

- You should almost always charge a fee, even if it's just $25. Your time is valuable, and you need to show people that you value your time. If an organization cannot pay you even a small speaking fee, chances are they might not value your time and message. (Keep in mind that this is for organizations hosting you. This rule in no way applies to book clubs or volunteer work you might do to boost your brand and spread your message. There are many times and situations where it will make sense for you to speak for free, and that is perfectly acceptable, too.)

- Include copies of your book with your speaking fee. Do your best to estimate how many people will be in attendance, and do your best to see to it that each of them leaves with a copy of your book.

- If you are selling your books before or after the event, be sure to have plenty of change and a working credit card reader. It is advisable to bring someone along to handle transactions while you sign books and greet people.

39

Should I be blogging?

Not necessarily. If you really don't want to or don't have the time to, then don't worry about blogging. You still, however, need a website—a good one that you update regularly.

The longer answer is . . . maybe. We are big fans of blogging (that's how Wise Ink started, after all). Blogging is a wonderful, free way to engage your audience and keep yourself relevant. We can never state enough that your juicy, value-rich content is what will sell your books. Creating new content (i.e. blog posts) is an ingenious way to remain visible to your current fans and attract new ones.

As with all things in book marketing, blogging will only be as worthwhile as the effort you put into it. Again, if the thought of blogging gives you anxiety, then skip it. But if you'd like to try it out, know that this does not have to be an enormous commitment. Sure, you could have a robust blog that funnels visitors into an email marketing list and is monetized using affiliate links, landing pages, and the like. Or you could have something more manageable. Either way, a blog is most effective when the blogger is committed to having fun and approaching it with the right strategy.

We believe that most books and authors make for successful blogs, but in case you are on the fence, here are a few ways to know if your book/brand would benefit from having a blog:

- If you are an expert in your field. (Assumedly, if you have written a book on a subject, you are an expert in it.)

- You have an audience that would benefit from supplemental information about your book.

- You can relate your book/brand material to current events.

- You have imagery that relates to your book.

- Your writing is humorous, you enjoy sharing your opinion, and your goal is to become a thought leader.

To know if you are a good candidate to become a blogger, answer these questions:

- Do you enjoy writing? (Don't laugh—this isn't always an easy answer!)

- Do you want to carve out a certain time to write, even if it's just a short piece?

- Are you willing to share these short pieces for free?

- Are you willing to promote your posts and respond to comments on them?

If the answers to the above questions are yes, we encourage you to blog. The following page contains a list of some dos and don'ts to make blogging manageable.

Do	Don't
• Keep your posts short, current, and sweet. Keep the polished essays for your portfolio, or submit those to larger publications.	• Expect immediate results. Building an audience with blogging takes time and persistence.
• Use images. Lots of images. (But don't steal them.) Canva is a great place to create blog graphics.	• Blog for the sake of blogging. A post that begins with, "I have no idea what to write today," isn't going to win you any fans. Be creative and positive.
• Write about topics that are relevant to you and your audience.	• Steal content. Be extremely careful to cite your sources and give credit where it is due.
• Create a manageable schedule. Bloggers who post more get the most traffic. Monthly won't cut it, so create a schedule that is as frequent as you can without diluting your content.	• Overshare. Be thoughtful about what you post, especially when it comes to your personal information.
• Share your posts. Facebook, Twitter, Linkedin, Pinterest—anywhere you have a social media presence.	• Tag people or post their pictures without their permission. Same goes for pictures of other people's children, obviously.
• Encourage people to subscribe to your blog. That will mean your blog posts will go directly to their inbox (and you will be able to have them on your ever-important email list). Often this is a quick add-on to your website that you can do yourself.	• Write anything provocative without being prepared for pushback. Putting out a controversial opinion is fine, but know that putting it out on social media opens you up to scrutiny.
• Run contests and promotions as part of your blogging efforts.	• Push people into sharing your posts. This includes tagging them in updates that say, "Friends, please share my latest blog!" This gets annoying fast.
• Encourage and respond to comments.	
• Boost your blog posts on social media. This is a great, cost-effective way to gain new followers and fans.	
• Read, follow, and comment on other people's blogs.	

Use this space to create a blogging schedule you think you can keep, as well as brainstorm ideas for topics to blog about:

Ideas for My Blog:

How do I host a giveaway?

First off, let's answer the question within this question: *Do I have to host give-aways?* The answer to this is no. Absolutely not. If you really don't want to give any of your books away, feel free to skip this section!

(To be clear, in this section we are talking about hosting giveaways with random winners, likely through social media. This is not to be confused with giving away copies of your books to bookstores and potential endorsers, which you absolutely should do.)

There are plenty of pros to giving away your book. It is a novel way to engage people on social media, a useful way to get your book noticed by a potential endorser, and a simple way to promote your book without being . . . well . . . annoying.

There is really only one con to hosting a giveaway, and that, of course, is that you are giving your book away. For free. And paying shipping! Convenient for the winner, less convenient for you.

Before hosting a giveaway, answer the following questions:

1. Am I okay with eating the cost of the books as well as shipping?

2. Am I okay with having my giveaway potentially not result in anything tangible, such as a positive book review or sale?

3. Am I willing to promote my giveaway on social media platforms, beyond my own friends and family?

If the answer to all three of these questions is yes, then you are set to host your giveaway!

First, brainstorm a few platforms to host your giveaway. We've listed some of the most obvious places here, but add more if you have them:

Platforms to host my giveaways through:

Facebook, Instagram, Twitter, LinkedIn, Goodreads, Amazon, your blog

Then, decide how many copies you'd like to give away. We suggest one to five copies, max, though you are welcome to give away as many as you like.

Next, create the draw. Think beyond a Facebook post that says, "I'm giving away a free copy of my book, comment and I'll pick a winner!"

Consider a few of these creative ideas:

- *To celebrate Mother's Day, I'm giving away one copy of my book,* Mom's Corner, *to a special mom. Comment with a few words to describe your mom and why she deserves a copy of my book!*

- *We are giving away one class set of my middle grade novel to one lucky charter school to promote a love of fiction. To enter, retweet and follow my Twitter page!*

- *The holidays are right around the corner! To celebrate, I'm giving away three copies of my fantasy novel. Tag two fantasy novel enthusiasts to enter!*

- *Need the perfect #summer beach read? Enter my #giveaway for one free copy of my book by replying with the hashtag #beachboundread*

Notice a few things about these examples:

1. They have a clear, celebratory message. "I'm giving away books because I'm really hoping to boost sales" is a terrible way of engaging an audience.

2. There is a win-win. People have to tag, retweet, reblog, etc. in order to enter. That gives your social media profiles a boost too.

3. There is clear, relevant engagement. If your book is tailored for dads, host a giveaway for Father's Day. If your book is poetry, host a giveaway to celebrate National Poetry Month. Use the momentum of a holiday as a natural partnership for your book.

4. These examples open the giveaway out to the public and force people to share your message with their followers in order to participate. You can, in theory, take all the entrants and invite them to follow you on social media or even purchase your book at a discounted price.

5. They are short and to the point. No one is going to read a long post about why you're giving books away and what they need to do to enter to win one. One to three sentences are plenty.

Brainstorm some messages here:

> ## My Giveaway Post Ideas:
>
> _____
>
> _____
>
> _____
>
> _____
>
> _____

Next, you'll want to create a graphic. No, you do not *need* a graphic. But yes, you want one. A visual is an important way to engage people. Luckily, you have a wonderful book cover that should do most of the talking!

If you are not graphic design-savvy, learn to use Canva. We love this easy-to-use software, which lets you create your own graphics for free.

Lastly, post!

As with all social media, be careful about promoting your giveaway. Once per day is enough. Do not overwhelm your followers with social media posts!

Important notes to consider:

- Giveaways on Goodreads are wonderful, but they have their own way of doing things. You will not need any sort of message or campaign to create a giveaway there. (As of January 2018, Goodreads is charging to host a giveaway. Keep this in mind as you plan your marketing budget.)

- Giveaways on Amazon are great, but you are limited to their system and ways of doing things.

- You must follow the rules of the social media site hosting the giveaway, and you do not want to learn these rules the hard way. For example, Facebook is very strict about not asking people to "follow" your page to enter a giveaway. (Doing so might result in getting your account taken down.)

- Be sure to connect with your winners! Send them your book, signed to them, and pro-actively thank them for reading *and* reviewing.

For social media graphic examples, visit wiseinkpub.com/authorresources

My book makes a perfect gift. What is the best way to market it around the holidays?

Books make perfect gifts, especially when they reach a person who really needs them. It's rare that we publish a book that we feel wouldn't make a good gift to the right reader.

As you begin brainstorming your marketing, factor who the perfect candidates are to receive your book as a gift. It's not enough to say, "My book makes the perfect holiday gift!" Clarify who your book would make the perfect holiday gift for. For some, the answer to this question will lead to a specific demographic—young women in college, dads over fifty, sports fans, spiritual seekers between thirty and fifty-five. However, we challenge you to also think about circumstances in which a person might need your book as a gift. For example, would your book work as a gift for someone who's experienced a loss—divorce, layoff, death? Or, on the positive side, could your book be given to someone starting a business, writing a book, exploring their spirituality, moving into a new home, or getting used to a recent promotion? The best and most thoughtful gifts are ones that source a need, complement a journey, or satisfy a hobby or healthy obsession.

Your book could also be a gift for an aspirational reader, such as someone looking to change careers, become a parent, scale a business, or travel the world. Brainstorm scenarios in which your book could be recommended as a gift for something or someone specific. This way, whether it's holiday season or not, your book can be gifted year round.

Here are a few questions to consider as you create a holiday marketing strategy. Use the right column to answer the questions for your book:

Question:	Answer:
Which holiday(s) make the most sense for me to market my book? (Think beyond Christmas. Research unique holidays that have to do with themes in your book that might be fun to piggyback on.)	
What can I pair my book with to make it a more appealing gift? (Think beyond a mug with your logo on it. What are some creative add-ons you can pair with your book? Can you partner with another author of a similar genre? Can you create a custom journal, a custom recipe card, or a unique trinket that would pair well with your book? Check out Pinterest and Etsy for inspiration!)	

Question:	Answer:
How can I personalize my book for a gift? (Maybe annotations or an offer to sign the books before sending them out?)	
Where are good places to showcase my gift set? (Gift shops are great, but can you also pursue other retail outlets like grocery stores or museums? What about doctors' and dentists' offices?)	
What is my strategy for promoting my book as a gift set online? (Start by blogging about who your book would make a perfect gift for; promote that post through your social media accounts and boost it. Who are allies who could support your promotion strategy?)	
How can I make my gift more appealing? (Free shipping is always nice, but can you do more? Maybe a BOGO offer?)	

Running a holiday deal can be as easy or as complicated as you want it to be. Generally speaking, we think the following are good rules to consider to make your holiday offer as successful (and hopefully sustainable) as possible:

- Do not operate at a loss. You should be making a profit on each sale.

- Consider your packaging carefully. Packaging can be very expensive and is a deep rabbit hole you can fall down if you're not careful. We have found a simple package works best.

- Partnerships are a wonderful way to engage your audience and reach more people.

- Do not offer a gift that is liquid or easily breakable. Save yourself that headache in shipping and transporting.

- Try and try again. Keep what works, skip what doesn't. Just because a promotion you run one time doesn't result in a lot of sales doesn't mean you should give up on it entirely.

What should I know about metadata?

We're glad you asked. Metadata is one of those topics that quickly—and rightfully so—garners yawns and heavy eyes from the crowd if you just so happen to be the lucky person tasked with giving an overview. Bear with us. We know it's not a favorite topic of authors. It's not a sexy subject by any stretch, and you might have even written it off as unimportant. We hope to change that. And here's why: Metadata can be the difference between your book showing up online correctly or not showing up at all. It's the reason some books catch your attention and *keep* your attention while other books barely get a first glance, much less a second. Metadata is what will help your book sell, and an absence of correct, complete metadata will stop your book from being successful. It is what Google, Amazon, Barnes & Noble, other retailers, search engines, and social media use to find your book and recommend it to readers. And since the internet is the main way readers shop, metadata is increasingly important for reaching your consumer.

So what do you need to know about metadata?

1. Simply put, metadata is information about your book data. It's your book information on steroids.

2. Effective metadata is discoverable.

If you don't carefully manage and update your Amazon author page, your vendor page, or your Goodreads profile, or even fill in all the relevant information when applying for an ISBN, you are making your book ambiguous. And ambiguity = lost sales.

Metadata is most useful to algorithms because algorithms like data . . . and lots of it. We are far from experts on this subject, especially as information about how algorithms work is always shifting and changing. We highly recommend reading *Let's Gets Visible* by David Gaughran, which gives the most thorough and simple overview of algorithms that we've come across. Your job as an author is to help algorithms discover your book as best you can. Even if you're working with a publisher, it's your job to ask what the process is for ensuring your book's metadata is submitted and crosschecked. In Metadata Land there are essentially two levels: basic and secondary.

Basic book metadata is:

- Title
- Subtitle
- Author
- Price
- Format (i.e. paperback, hardcover, audiobook, ebook)
- ISBN

This is pretty simple; you should know all these details and can complete this information accurately. Basic metadata is the primary data pulled into databases across the Internet and most commonly scrutinized by libraries, retailers, and book information websites like Bowker. The next level of metadata requires more thoughtful execution:

- Book Description
- Category
- Keywords
- Target Audience

When it comes to secondary metadata, keep the following things in mind:

1. **Book Description.** Your book's description should feature several keywords integral to your book's topic, including any phrases you think a reader would search for on Amazon or in a search engine.

2. **Category.** This is not exactly the same as your book genre. For example, your book might be shelved in a bookstore under "Literature." However, for more specificity, you might use the BISAC code FIC022110, which is for cozy mysteries featuring cats and dogs. Most traditional book distributors will use BISAC codes—which you can find a full list of at www.bisg.org—but Amazon uses its own categories.

3. **Keywords.** Think of Amazon as a search engine. Your book's keywords are really most important here—without good keywords, your book won't show up in searches. For fiction, keywords are likely to be a combination of settings, themes, genre, imagery, symbolism, and key character attributes. For nonfiction, keywords are likely to be topics, ideas, phrases in the book, and audience attributes. (A few keywords for this book are: *self-publishing, book marketing, how-to market books, author marketing, Amazon tips for authors.*) Look through your book and note the most-used words and phrases throughout. These are often the words that aren't thought of as keywords, but should be.

4. **Target audience.** Your target audience is important for retailers, and often for media. The more specific you can get, the better. Refer to chapter 8 for our take on defining your target audience.

43

Do I need an audiobook? What are the pros and cons of having one?

You absolutely don't *need* an audiobook. But for certain books—memoirs, spiritual and inspirational titles, and fiction—an audiobook can increase overall sales.

The biggest downside to creating an audiobook is that it can be pricey. There are several ways to create audiobooks, but the easiest way we have found is using ACX, Amazon's Audiobook Creation Exchange. The cost is roughly $200 or more per finished hour of work. A 100,000-word manuscript is about eleven hours of audio, meaning over a $2000 investment.

If this investment is too much for you, skip this section. After all, audiobooks are not an immediate need.

If you do have the funds but don't know if this is a good investment for you, the following page has a helpful pro/con list to consider before taking the plunge:

Think about creating an audiobook if:	Skip the audiobook if:
• Your readers are big consumers of audiobooks. This might be hard to gauge, so do some digging on your own. Use the platform you've built and ask how many of those readers are listeners of audiobooks. We see many genre fiction books on the bestseller lists for audiobooks but hardly any children's books, for example.	• You are way over-budget on marketing. Creating an audiobook will in no way guarantee sales. You'll have to sell a lot of audiobooks to even recover your investment.
• You have written a memoir or a self-help book. Both genres have the feel of an author truly speaking to the reader. Having your voice narrate the audiobook could be a very appealing selling point.	• You are not a consumer of audiobooks yourself. If you don't listen to audiobooks, how will you know if yours will lend itself well to that format?
• Your book has a performance element to it that lends itself well to being read aloud. If you have very stylized characters, for example, who could be voiced by a professional voice actor, an audiobook might be a good idea.	• You are unable or unwilling to promote the audiobook as a new, enhanced, or exciting version of your book that people should buy. We could never repeat this enough: any marketing you do for your book, especially marketing that has a large price tag, will only be effective if you are willing to promote it yourself.
• Your book could be enhanced by an "extra" feature—maybe an interview with you, a musical enhancement or soundtrack, or some other feature that a person couldn't get otherwise.	• Your audiobook will simply be someone narrating your story. This is fine, don't get us wrong. But assuming you are doing this on your own and don't have unlimited access to funds, don't create an audiobook for the sake of creating one. As with all things, have a strategy.

44

Now that I'm an author, should I join my local literary community?

It depends on your genre. If you have written a book of poetry or literary fiction, you certainly should be ingrained in your local literary community. If you have written a business book or other nonliterary, niche title (meaning your audience isn't necessarily picking up your book for its literary merit) there are likely other communities more valuable to you.

Depending on where you live, your literary community could look any number of ways. Here are a few places to start getting connected locally:

- Community centers
- Art centers, museums, and theaters
- Independent bookstores
- Gift shops and large booksellers such as Barnes & Noble
- Literary magazines (find these in the libraries in your area)
- Facebook (search "events near me")
- Eventbrite (search literary events in your zip code)

Use this area to write down the literary organizations or publications in your community.

My local literary community organizations, publications, and events:

_____

_____

_____

_____

_____

_____

_____

_____

_____

_____

_____

If you are in a very rural area or you simply can't find any literary organizations to take part in, consider creating one yourself. It could be as easy as a monthly reading at a local coffee shop.

Your literary community is likely always looking for readers and speakers. We suggest approaching the organizer with a personal email, maybe a press release, and a pitch to feature you. Remember to align your pitch to the vision of the event, not the vision of your small business as an author.

Here are a few tips to keep in mind when reading at a literary event:

- Have books to sell, but don't push sales. People coming to a reading are coming to be entertained, not to hear a sales pitch. If they love your work, they will buy your book.

- Keep your reading short and sweet. An excerpt from your book is fine, but use an excerpt that works well as a standalone sample of your book—choose an excerpt that won't get lost in translation. If the organizer gives you five minutes, read for no more than five minutes.

- Practice. Practice. Practice. No matter how comfortable you think you are in front of a crowd, if you don't practice your reading, it will show.

- Have business cards ready for those who want to connect with you after your reading.

- Connect with people. This is your opportunity to make friends, support others on their writing journey, and connect with influential people in your area. Use the opportunity wisely.

- Have fun and don't take yourself too seriously. We completely understand that reading at a literary event can be daunting, but this is what it's all about. Your story should be heard, and you should be proud to tell it!

How do I market my book if I cannot travel?

There are a million reasons a person might be unable to travel to promote their book. The good news for any author who is homebound for any reason is that social media has really leveled the playing field for authors speaking to their readers directly. Using social media wisely can market your book, no matter what your personal circumstances are.

Here are a few of our favorite ways authors who cannot travel outside the home can make the most of their situation and still market their books:

Teach a class remotely

We are always pushing authors to create and host events as a way to connect to potential readers and selling books. Thankfully, online classes are gaining in popularity and are an equally effective way to reach a crowd and earn serious revenue. Explore opportunities to work with your local community center, community college, or literary center to see about pitching an online class. Also, check out Udemy and Teachable as two online platforms for launching a course.

Host and participate in online chats

Online chats are a wonderful way of connecting with your audience from the comfort of your home. Twitter chats in particular are often well-planned and simple to jump in and out of with the correct hashtag. While it's fun to connect with other writers this way, keep in mind that you'll also want to join chats to engage your audience.

Offer to visit classrooms, organizations, and book clubs using video conferencing tools like Skype, Google Hangouts, and Zoom

Video conferencing works wonderfully for virtual presentations and allows you to participate in remote events like Q&A discussions and interviews. Be sure to promote this as a way you are willing to connect with readers using your social media platforms. Also, consider sharing your availability for virtual events by sending an email blast to your mailing list.

Consider a blog tour

Blog tours with the right partners can lead to online buzz. Several companies can "host" these tours for you, and you pay for their service based on the amount of "stops" you have. (See chapter 31 for more information.)

Cross-promote, guest post, and make as many online "friends" as possible

We are always delighted by the amount of support we see, particularly online, for indie authors. If you are homebound, use the time you might have spent pounding the pavement to scour the web for partnerships. Seek bloggers already serving your audience and approach them with win-win partnership ideas, which may include promoting products they offer in exchange for posting a guest blog. Offer free PDFs of your book in exchange for a review. Be a positive and responsive online presence.

Use this space to brainstorm blogs, virtual classes, and online chats you can participate in:

Opportunities and ideas to reach my readers remotely:

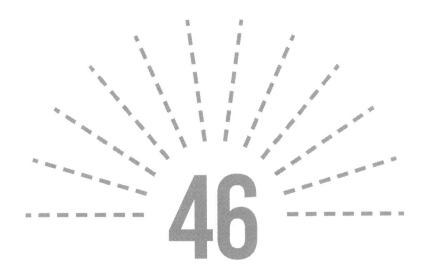

46

What are the right events to attend as an author?

The list could be long or longer depending on your marketing plan, big picture goals, and your book's audience. If you follow other authors on social media (and you absolutely should), you'll see plenty of posts about events—festivals, conferences, workshops, panels, discussions, and readings. The reason most authors fill their calendar with these events is ultimately to sell books. But where do you start? How do you know which events to attend? Are they all worth it?

Here's the deal. Once you publish your book, you could fill every Saturday and Sunday for an entire year with events where you have a table, sell your book, network, and meet incredible people. But let's be honest—you don't want to expend all of your energy, time, and money going to everything.

We have found that events are often hit or miss. For every amazing holiday market where an author has sold a hundred books, there is another holiday market where an author has sat in a mostly empty room for half a day. And many events aren't free—almost every event has a fee attached to it, not to mention the time investment of spending an entire day away from home.

We suggest setting an event goal for yourself each year. Four or five selling events are plenty. You'll want to choose events that are:

- **Credible.** If the event is hosted by a group you've never heard of, in a space you've never heard of, and for an occasion you haven't heard of, these are all red flags that the event might not be a good use of time.

- **Well-promoted.** Before paying for a table at an event, check out Facebook and Eventbrite to be sure an event has been created, is open to the public, and is being promoted across platforms.

- **Reasonably priced.** Some conferences are more expensive to attend than others, but keep in mind that spending a thousand dollars for a table at a literary festival means selling tons of books just to break even. Ask yourself if the risk is worth it.

- **Attractive to your readers.** We cannot stress this enough. You know your audience. Will they be in attendance? And more importantly, will they be willing to spend money there?

Use this space to dig into events that you want to take part in for your book. Start locally, contact the organizer, and make sure you think of ways to draw your readers to your table (and then to hopefully buy your book).

Event	Contact	Date(s)	Display Ideas

47

What should I do if
I get a bad book review?

Celebrate. Seriously, congratulations! You've made it through the long, difficult process of independent publishing. You've written and revised your book, gotten feedback from beta readers, worked with an experienced editor and proofreader, and created a kickass cover and interior with the right book design professional. You've navigated the world of social media, and you've created a marketing plan. In short, you've done a big, scary, amazing thing, and people all over the country (and maybe even the world) are probably going to buy your book.

Depending on your genre, your readers might hang out on sites like Goodreads, where they can recommend and write reviews of books. Or maybe they just want to share their opinions on Amazon or other online booksellers' sites. If a review of your book is positive, it can help bolster sales, and more people will be willing to take the plunge and purchase it too. But there's one thing to remember: once word starts to spread about your book, no matter how good it is, you will get bad reviews. Enjoy all the five-star reviews that are constructive and that might even help with your next projects. You'll receive plenty of those.

You'll also get a few bad reviews. Thanks to the dreaded internet troll, who just likes to stir up controversy and make people angry, or to the person who genuinely did not like your book, you will get a negative review eventually.

When faced with a trolling bad review, it's tempting to defend yourself or try and get that review taken down. When you get a bit of constructive criticism, it's tempting to respond and say thank you or explain your writing choices.

But don't do any of these things.

Bad reviews aren't as damning as you might think. In fact, they work to legitimize your good reviews, and most savvy internet users are able to sniff out a troll from a mile away, so they won't give much credence to those reviews.

Even though your book is your baby, defending it might make you appear unlikable, ungrateful, and like you have nothing better to do. Explaining why you wrote something a particular way could come across as argumentative and defensive.

Does a bad review hurt? Yep. Shake it off and focus on the positive. Tuck it away in your mind as a reason to keep writing, to keep improving. Make bad reviews a source of motivation to get more good ones. You'll get there soon enough.

48

Will high book sales help me get a book deal?

If there were a magic formula for getting a book deal, we would happily pass that formula on to you. When people think of book deals, they are usually thinking about the six-figure ones that get national attention. Often, those deals go to people who already have enormous platforms, pages of accolades, and a well-known name.

If that is you, write a book for the rest of us about your journey to get there.

If that is not you, then you have work ahead of you to secure a book deal, *if* this is even your goal to begin with. And yes, a lot of that work is going to involve selling books, establishing a content-rich platform, and becoming an authority figure in your subject matter *without* the backing of a huge publisher.

That's a lot of work. Also, once you do all that hard work, you might find that the benefits of a large royalty publisher aren't as necessary.

The truth is that even if you used this book to sell ten thousand copies of your novel, checked all the right marketing boxes, established a platform, and hired the world's savviest publicist, there are no guarantees you would get a book deal. And even if you did get a book deal, it would likely not be a six-figure deal.

But does selling high numbers of books open the door for a publishing deal down the line? It can't hurt. The bottom line, book deal or not, is that building your fanbase and marketing yourself well—and often—is the key to opening all the doors of further opportunity, book deal or otherwise.

What should I do when sales start to go stale?

First things first: relax. When you decided to become an author, you—perhaps unknowingly—chose a path wrought with ups and downs. It's the nature of the beast. There will be times that you will look at your past months of sales, then look at your inventory, and have a bit of a panic attack. That's okay. You are not a failure. Your book doesn't suck. You shouldn't regret publishing.

For many authors, this moment of reckoning comes about six months after their book's launch. The party is over, the first big rounds of signings are done, the "buzz" has started to get a bit quieter. And yet you still have books to sell. We get it. That is scary stuff.

But it's not the end of the world. Here are a few ways to re-engage and hopefully reignite sales when they go stale:

- **Write a provocative blog post.** What's been your best or worst experience in publishing? What popular myth about your book/genre/life can you debunk? Pitch that blog post to *HuffPost*, your favorite blog, or a popular website that takes submissions, or post it to your website and promote it.

- **Create an event.** Consider hosting a Facebook Live chat; a class at your local community center about the craft of writing or on one of your book's topics; or a Twitter chat. Create an event centered on something larger than selling copies of your book. Engage your audience through creating captivating content.

- **Participate in an existing Twitter chat.** Find a hashtag that engages your readers and proactively join Twitter conversations.

- **Contact your local bookstore or library for a speaking or signing event.** Again, start a conversation about a topic bigger than your book. Sell you. What can you do to bring people into that bookstore or library to see you?

- **Get creative.** Think about unique ways to get in front of your audience. Send copies of your book to a few people outside your circle. Ask your friends if they know of some book clubs that might be interested in reading your book. Find events your readers might participate in and think of swag you can pass out to get people interested in your book. The possibilities are endless.

Brainstorm your ideas here:

My Re-Launching Marketing Ideas:

50

How will I know when my book has run its course?

If you're asking this question, you are likely in one of two categories: you are either debating a reprint of your book, or are sitting on inventory that hasn't moved in a long time. The latter is a much tougher place to be, so we will address the easier situation first.

Reprints are a significant milestone you can leverage to generate fresh buzz for your book, especially if you're adding new or updated content to its pages. Think of a reprint as an opportunity to have a mini-launch. You can add an award emblem to your cover, a foreword from a stakeholder with name recognition, and a page with an updated list of the glowing reviews you've received. You can even have a relaunch party.

While you will be going into a reprint situation with your eyes much more open as to how the whole process works, keep in mind that after that reprint happens, you will need to start a lot of this marketing work over again. Chances are, if you've sold two thousand copies of your book, you have also tapped out certain networks. Be willing to branch out even further with a reprint.

In other words, get back on the treadmill.

Now, for the tougher question. *What do I do when I've done all of this and I still can't move my inventory? How do I know when to call it a day, cut my losses, and move on?*

Of course, only you can answer that question. But before you donate twenty-five boxes of books to the nearest Goodwill and spend the rest of your life lamenting your failed writing career, we invite you to reflect on these questions:

Question:	Answer:
Have I truly utilized all my marketing connections, or have I just reached out to the ones that felt the most comfortable?	
Have I reached far and wide on social media to see what organizations I can partner with to get my message out?	
What has worked for me, and what hasn't? How can I rework the marketing campaigns that have been successful for me, mix them up, and try them again?	

Question:	Answer:
Am I really "over" being a writer, or do I just need a break from the intense work of marketing?	
Does my book have mistakes in it, a poor design, or outdated content that could be hurting my sales? Should I consider a redesign or reedit?	

Finally, we invite you to reflect back on the first exercise in this book, the one where you defined what success means to you. You are either doing the work toward those goals or you are not. Simply put, the writing work is "over" when you stop trying.

There might be a time when you decide for any number of reasons that you are not going to be marketing your work anymore. That is okay. But we hope that you come to a place of knowing—no matter how many books you've sold—that you have found success. You wrote a book; a book that likely impacted lives for the better. You realized a dream, and the people in your life saw you do it. And maybe your bravery inspired someone else to realize their dreams, too.

No matter what has brought you to this last chapter, your writing career has been a phenomenal success. And that, we feel, deserves a celebration.

CONCLUSION: YOU GOT THIS

Recently at the office, we were having a delightful conversation about parenting. How fantastic, frightening, beautiful, rewarding, exhausting, and terrible it can be. If you're a parent or have been parented you know how tough it is to be responsible for a human. In this conversation, one mom recalled a particular moment of terror when being discharged from the hospital, newborn baby in tow. You see, those couple days after giving birth, you're in a lovely cocoon of safety and support—nurses, doctors, and visitors by your side gleefully stepping in to hold your hand (and baby) as you bond with your new human. When you have questions, someone is there to answer them. When you're tired, frustrated, or plain overwhelmed, there's a person ready to assist. It's rare to contemplate in those moments, the specifics of "ever after."

The newness of becoming a parent is intense, how could you possibly focus on anything else? It's almost like there's a conspiracy to entrap new parents in the euphoria of those precious first days so that when things get super hard—and they will—you're in so deep that no dark moment could possibly alter the love you have for your kid. We all agreed how frightening it felt leaving the hospital. "I mean, you actually trust me to keep this kid alive?" one mom exasperatedly asked her doctor, who then replied, "Yep. You got this."

It's trite at this point to compare birthing a book to birthing a child, yet the parallels are hard to ignore. After being in the trenches creating your incredible book, hopefully, with support and encouragement, you likely feel a bit of fear. Hear us when we say: of course, you do. Fear is normal. Building a platform requires time and patience. Like every new parent, you'll lose your way. Remember your why. When you find yourself running out of ideas. No biggie. Most authors, even famous ones, all experience that at one point or another.

You are learning as you go, as you should. And your path is yours alone. Own it! We can't tell you exactly what the next chapter looks like. There's no way to know. But we do know that every effort you make to get your book into the hands of readers who need it, means more readers you're going to touch, lives you're going to impact, and doors that will open for you. The possibilities are truly endless. Good luck, friend. Trust us when we say: You got this.

APPENDIX A

Sample Marketing Calendar

This is probably why you grabbed this book, right? A marketing calendar you could just cut and paste and use for yourself?

We have good news and bad news. Let's start with the bad news: There is no marketing calendar that is ready to use right out of the box. Your marketing plan should be customized and empower immediate results. But you should know this already if you've read this book!

The good news is that, although a marketing calendar sounds like an enormous project, it doesn't have to be terribly complex. Here is a sample we used for this book, which you are welcome to take, change, and customize for your own purposes. It is essentially a checklist, and yes, some of these items required their own checklists. But we are here to tell you that if you can take it step by step, you won't feel overwhelmed by all there is to do!

Goals

(Make a list of at least three tangible goals for your launch and beyond. Everything you do for your book's marketing should have a direct correlation to at least one of these goals. If you are considering a marketing opportunity that does not directly correlate to one of your goals, skip it!)

- Sell five thousand copies of *Buzz: 50 Book Marketing Questions Every Author Should Ask*

- Increase our social media following across all platforms by 50 percent

- Host at least three book marketing events in 2019

- Enter and win three award competitions

Six Months from Launch

(This work should start after the book is written and while it is being edited. Keep in mind that content sells your book; you need to create content that will engage your potential audience and posit yourself as an authority on your subject.)

- Contact possible endorsers

- Create purchase links on our website for the book

- Determine email marketing campaign (see sample)

- Determine content calendar (see sample)

Three Months from Launch

(This is the time to focus on your launch event. Make it organic to you. Set up a venue, consider people to come speak at your event, or even partner with a local artist to make the event a win-win. Remember that the launch will likely be your biggest "push" for your event. Everything you do should be focused on creating buzz!)

- Determine logistics for book launch (this will likely be a multistep process, so take time!)

- Obtain an editorial review from *Kirkus*

- Contact local bookstores about purchasing our book to sell on consignment

- Hire a publicist

- Create ten graphics to use on social media highlighting the positive reviews we've received

One Month from Launch

(Assuming your launch event is secure, use the final four weeks to spread the word. If you have a publicist, they should be hard at work securing press for you. If you are doing your own publicity, now is the time!)

- Have the publicist draft the first press release and determine outlets to distribute it

- Create the book launch event and promote it through Facebook

- Create and print "extras" for book launch

- Post about Buzz on all social media platforms three times per week

Launch

(Your launch event should be a celebration. Enjoy it! You deserve this!)

- Have someone Facebook Live our launch event

- Take photos of people holding a copy of *Buzz* at our launch event

Post-Launch

- Post photos taken at the launch event to social media, one image per week

- Create one blog post per month highlighting a question from the *Buzz* book

- Set up three book marketing courses via community ed, The Loft, and The Coven

- Set up a Facebook and Twitter ad campaign to sell *Buzz* online

Sample Content Calendar

Content calendars can be as simple or as complex as you want them to be. We feel strongly that content sells your book far better than an ad or a plea on Facebook or Twitter, so taking the time to create a content calendar that makes sense for you and your book is extremely important. Here is an example of a content calendar we share with our authors of many genres that would be timely and totally manageable, not to mention customizable for your own platform.

January	February	March
New Year *Inspiration* *Goal Setting*	*Black History Month* *Superbowl* *Valentine's Day* *Random Act of Kindness Week*	*National Reading Month* *International Women's Day* *Employee Appreciation Day*
• Your writing resolutions • Five tips for authors about any aspect of the writing process • Books that have inspired you • Your reading goals for 2018	• Black authors who have inspired you or your writing • Sports figures who have inspired you or your writing • Your favorite love story • Maybe a promotion to give your book as a random act of kindness?	• Your favorite books of all time • Women who have inspired your writing • Your favorite female author(s) • Your favorite female protagonist

April	May	June
National Library Week *Earth Day* *Indie Bookstore Day*	*Mother's Day* *National Teacher Appreciation Day* *Memorial Day*	*Father's Day* *Summer Reading*
• Memories of your own childhood library • How you support your public library • Your favorite indie bookstore • Photos of you and/or your book in an indie bookstore	• Your favorite gift books for mom • Your favorite gift books for teachers • Veterans who have inspired you and your writing • How your mother has influenced your work	• Your favorite gift books for dad • Father figures in literature who have inspired you • Your summer reading list (pick a genre) • Interview another author about their writing process or favorite book(s)

July	August	September
Summer Reading	*Summer Reading*	*Grandparents Day* *Back to School*
• Your summer reading list (pick another genre) • Something about your craft—how do YOU write? • Interview another author • Create a graphic celebrating your book	• Your summer reading list (pick another genre) • Your favorite authors to follow on social media • Five things you've learned by publishing a book • Some sort of "end of summer" special	• How have/had your grandparents influenced your writing journey? • Your favorite book from high school • Five things that have surprised you about publishing a book • "Back to school" special

October	November	December
Boss's Day *Make a Difference Day*	*Veteran's Day* *Thanksgiving*	*Holiday Push!* *Support small business and indie authors!*
• How are you using your book to make a difference in the world? • Your favorite reads about the workplace • Your favorite books that make a difference • Highlight an author making a difference in your community	• What are you grateful for as a writer? • How important is gratitude in the writer's life? • Who/what are your muses, and why? • Can you personally call out people who have been supportive of you as a writer?	• Small business Saturday—the importance of buying from small businesses! • Your favorite indie books of the year • Indie writers you are excited about • A holiday push—BOGO, free shipping, etc!

APPENDIX C

Sample Email Marketing Campaign

As we know from our friend Tim Grahl, the expert in all things book marketing, your email list is your number-one resource when it comes to marketing your book. An email marketing campaign might seem like a lot of work, but it's not! Check out our sample email marketing campaign for *Buzz*.

Before starting an email marketing campaign:

- Set up MailChimp or another email service

- Decide on a time/email duration (we decided on one email per month for the six months leading to the launch, and then a follow-up email after the launch)

- Decide on an email template you can easily use time and again

- Create graphics for each and every email

- Ensure all links to your website for purchase or event registration are active before posting

Six-Month Email Marketing Campaign Sample:

Month 1
Subject: Does My Business Need a Book?
Text: Interview questions with Wise Ink author John Wessinger about how his business has been strengthened by his book
Graphic: *Buzz Book: Coming Soon*

Month 2

Subject: What Should I Do When I'm Running Out of Writing Steam?

Text: Interview questions with Wise Ink author Jennifer Rock about prioritizing writing time

Graphic: *Buzz Book: Coming Soon*

Month 3

Subject: Should I Let People Read a Rough Draft of My Book?

Text: Interview questions with Russell Ricard about the drafting/beta reader process and what works for him

Graphic: *Buzz Book: Coming Soon*

Month 4

Subject: How Do I Make My Book Stand Out?

Text: Interview questions with Wise Ink author TJ Tison about setting her book apart from the competition

Graphic: *Buzz preorder graphic/link*

Month 5

Subject: Do I Really Need to Be on Social Media?

Text: Interview with Wise Ink author Angela Miller about her use of social media

Graphic: *Buzz Book: Preorder and Launch Party*

Month 6

Subject: How Do I Throw a Phenomenal Launch Party?

Text: Interview with Wise Ink author Tera Girardin about her launch event

Graphic: *Book Book: Preorder and Launch Party*

Final email: Thank-you to all who came/supported the event, link for purchase, special discount code

101 Ways to Market Your Book

1. Create a marketing plan

2. Research your readers' favorite websites, blogs, and social media platforms

3. Conduct a focus group with potential buyers

4. Craft your elevator pitch

5. Create business cards

6. Create a sell sheet for your book

7. Create a media kit that includes a press release, Q&A sheet, bio, and sell sheet

8. Launch your website

9. Publish blogs to your website

10. Become a guest blogger

11. Register for conferences

12. Go to a book fair

13. Network with other writers

14. Collect email addresses at events

15. Create an email opt-in option for your blog or website

16. Bring books to your local library

17. Announce your book in your college alumni publication

18. Run targeted social media ads

19. Buy ad space on a blog or website

20. Create a Facebook page

21. Create a Twitter account

22. Reply to and retweet other authors

23. Research the hashtags that are important to your reader

24. Record a video blog post

25. Upload a video to YouTube

26. Create book club discussion questions

27. Add your social media handles to your bio on your book

28. Offer your book as a raffle item at a conference

29. Offer to create a gift basket for your favorite nonprofit's gala silent auction—add your book to it

30. Publish articles to LinkedIn

31. Send updates, news, and resources to your email list

32. Start a monthly newsletter

33. Create a coupon code for buyers who purchase from your website

34. Profile and highlight your favorite books

35. Profile and highlight your favorite authors

36. Profile and highlight your favorite readers

37. Start an affiliate program

38. Ask your network to recommend your book

39. Ask your network to post pictures of themselves with your book

40. Join the Goodreads Author Program

41. Create an Amazon Author Central account

42. Give discounts for bulk orders

43. Partner with a store or brand on an event

44. Join a professional organization

45. Plan your next holiday promotion

46. Launch a free webinar or workshop

47. Record a podcast

48. Schedule your social media post ahead of time

49. Teach a class at your local arts center

50. Hire an intern

51. Get on Reddit

52. Create infographics and pin them to Pinterest

53. Post beautiful pics of your book on Instagram

54. Tease your next book

55. Give away the first chapter

56. Network with book reviewers and book bloggers online

57. Run a contest on Instagram or Facebook

58. Apply for book awards

59. Throw a book launch party

60. Have a business-card drawing at events—give a free book to the winner

61. Add "author" to your LinkedIn, Twitter, Instagram, and Facebook profiles

62. Encourage readers to post reviews to Amazon

63. Know your book's keywords

64. Relaunch your book with a refreshed cover

65. Craft a catchy elevator pitch

66. Launch a crowdfunding campaign

67. Make your book available for pre-orders

68. Post a cover reveal on a popular blog

69. Set up a NetGalley account

70. Offer free copies to Amazon top reviewers

71. Run book giveaways on Goodreads, a blog tour, or Facebook

72. Ask readers to review your book in its back matter

73. Submit your book to publications for reviews (*RT Book Reviews* and *Kirkus*)

74. Add a free ebook sampler to retailer sites

75. Add an excerpt to Wattpad

76. Sell themed merchandise on your website to your most loyal fans (e.g. T-shirts)

77. Discount a backlist book to drive sales

78. Discount the first book in your series

79. Make your first book in a series free across all platforms to serve as a gateway to the rest of the series

80. Submit a post to Buzzfeed

81. Optimize your social media posts with images (e.g. your book cover, a teaser quote, etc.)

82. Schedule your social media posts using a resource like Buffer, Hootsuite, or TweetDeck

83. Host a virtual party on Facebook

84. Create Pinterest boards of inspiration

85. Snap behind-the-scenes photos and post to Instagram

86. Stream a Facebook Live video

87. Host a Q&A discussion or chat on Twitter

88. Post articles to Medium

89. Host a Q&A via Snapchat and YouTube

90. Create an author fan club

91. Launch a Facebook group with other authors

92. Publish a multi-author anthology

93. Participate on panels

94. Concentrate marketing efforts in a single week

95. Pitch your book as a holiday gift

96. Regularly refresh your metadata with updated keywords on Amazon

97. Write the next book

98. Advertise your book on Amazon

99. Create a pop-up shop at a non-book-oriented venue (e.g. museum, outdoor festival, grocery store, coffee shop, marathon, etc.)

100. Thank one fan a week on your social media platforms

101. Turn your book into a course or workshop

GLOSSARY

affiliate arrangement: Affiliate arrangements are essentially partnerships. For example, on Amazon, if you were an affiliate ("associate" in Amazon-speak), it means that you would "endorse" key products on your blog or website that are linked to your brand and in turn earn money when someone clicked on the link on your website and went back to the Amazon site.

ARC: Advanced reader copies, also known as galleys, are physical copies of your book printed in advance of your launch. ARCs are used to generate buzz for your book and acquire reviews and endorsements. ARCs are optional.

blitz: In the publishing world, a blitz often refers to some sort of timed push you do for your book. You could do a blitz where you have all your friends review your book on Amazon at one time, you could do a "media blitz" where you and your publicist work to get you interviewed in as many places as possible during a certain time, or you could even do a "blitz" around a giveaway.

brand: Your brand as an author is the overall professional profile you maintain. Your genre, writing style, and speaking style are all a part of your brand, as well as anything you print or post on social media. Being conscious of your brand while also not being overly contrived about it is one of the hardest parts of being an author, and it takes practice and confidence!

content calendar: A schedule of "content" you are going to be posting on social media, whether that be Facebook, Instagram, your blog, or some other platform. We have found that having a calendar of content not only keeps your posts fresh and engaging, it also prevents authors from burning out or becoming stuck.

consignment: Consignment means that someone, maybe a bookstore or gift shop owner, is selling a small amount of your books and will pay you for the purchase of those books if and when they sell. If they don't sell during a certain amount of time, you will be responsible for picking them up from the store. If they do sell, you'll be responsible for restocking the vendor.

crowdfunding: A good way to raise the money to publish your book is by crowdfunding using Kickstarter or Indiegogo. We highly recommend making sure that your campaigns on a crowdfunding platform include visuals of the book itself, so keep in mind that you will likely be using a crowdfunding campaign to pay yourself back or pay for one of your last indie author expenses: printing. Crowdfunding is also an excellent way to gather preorders!

demographics: When it comes to your audience, identifying your demographics, or data around your reading population, is really important. Knowing information about your readers, such as where they shop for books and what social media platforms they frequent, can be invaluable in terms of targeting them for ads and promotions for your book.

distribution: Distribution refers to the channel through which your book is going to get into the hands of readers and bookstores. Some authors work with a warehouse that fulfills orders to booksellers and wholesalers while some serve as their own distributors, working directly with bookstores and selling directly to readers.

distribution house: The actual warehouse where your books will be stored, such as Ingram or Baker & Taylor. These distribution houses will supply books to Amazon to fulfill orders, as well as take orders for your book directly.

email list: An email list is a list of people who might be interested in buying your book. Creating and maintaining your email list is very important, as email is a great way to communicate with your readers. You'll want to collect email addresses everywhere you go and use a service such as Mailchimp to send emails to them: that way people can opt out of your emails if they want to.

endorsements: Endorsements are quotes from influential people about how much they love you or your book. Unlike a general review, an endorsement should carry some weight with your audience and be from someone with either name or title recognition. You can never have too many endorsements!

engagement: When it comes to being an author, engagement has to do with communication. Retweets, likes, pins—all these are ways that readers can engage with you on social media (and you can engage with them!) Indie authors in particular should be engaging with their readers and potential readers regularly, either through social media, email, or speaking events.

galley: see *ARC*

hashtag: Think of a hashtag as a way of organizing subjects. For example, if you are a cooking blogger, you might post to social media with hashtags such as #breakfast or #homecook. Similarly, you'll notice that we will be on social media promoting this book with hashtags like #bookmarketing or #indieauthor. People hop on certain social media platforms, such as Twitter, and search hashtags that interest them, so it's important to use relevant hashtags whenever possible.

launch: Your launch date is technically the date your book is available for purchase, namely through Amazon or some other distributor. Your launch event (or events!), usually held around the same time, is the event that you plan to celebrate the release of your book.

metadata: Metadata is information you get from other data. For an author, metadata often refers to information gleaned from data about your book sales. For example, if you have one bookstore that is constantly running out of copies of your book, you might have metadata saying that the people who frequent that bookstore love your genre. Similarly, if you look at the analytics from your website, you'll likely discover lots of valuable metadata.

opt-in box: an opt-in box is one of those little pop-up boxes you see on someone's website asking for your email. When you give it, you're "opting in" to email updates from that site. This is extremely valuable! You can also use an opt-in box in exchange for free content people download from your website.

pitch: A pitch is essentially a formal presentation or "ask" of someone else. For example, if you'd like to host an event at a certain place or ask someone for an endorsement, the way you approach them is called a pitch. Similarly, a publicist is paid to "pitch" you, your book, and your message when you hire them.

platform: You'll hear authors talk about "platform" all the time, and for good reason. Think of your platform as the building blocks you have leading people to you and your book. Your author platform is comprised of your social media presence, your branding, and all of your events and marketing around being an author. The larger and more engaging your platform, the more success you'll likely see.

press kit: A a collection of documents used by a publicist (or yourself) to pitch you and your book. A press kit normally contains a press release, an author Q&A, a sell sheet, an excerpt from your book, and any other "handout" that might be useful for media.

press release: A press release is probably one of the most important elements of your press kit. It should include the cover of your book, relevant purchasing and launch information, and a "story" about how your book has launched, what it's about, and why it's important. In theory, a media outlet will receive your press release and have enough information to create a story about you.

print-on-demand: POD is a great option for printing and distributing indie books. When someone purchases your book via Amazon, the book is printed when the order is placed and then shipped to the customer. On the plus side, this can take away the cost of printing a large quantity of books and/or sitting on inventory. On the negative side, however, printing on-demand means indie authors receive far less profit per sale.

print run: Your print run is how many books you print at a time. When you launch, you'll have an "initial" print run. Print Run is also an awesome podcast hosted by Wise Ink's own Laura Zats!

profiles (social media): Your profile is the "page" you have on a social media site, which includes your pictures, banners, and text. As an author, you will need to carefully maintain your social media profiles and be sure to engage with people who ask you questions or review your books there there!

promotion: Promoting your book or event is essentially advertising it. While you should definitely be working on promoting yourself (self-promotion), we have found that the best way to promote your book or event is through partnerships. For example, if you pitch yourself for an event at a bookstore and that bookstore promotes you through their social media, and you in turn promote that bookstore through YOUR social media, that is cross-promotion. Win-win!

publicist: A publicist is a professional who promotes and pitches you to media. Publicists often have extensive media contact lists and should be heavily connected in the community. Publicist rates vary based on offerings and experience.

sell sheet: A sell sheet is similar to a press release. It will usually contain the same type of information (book cover, summary, endorsement, purchase info, etc.) but is typically much brighter and more colorful to attract the attention of a potential buyer. Sell sheets can be made and handed out or attached in emails indiscriminately.

sponsorships: A sponsorship in the author world is when a company pays for a portion of your book creation or distribution fees in exchange for something, such as a custom printing to include their logo or a special discount on a bulk order.

vendor: A vendor is an entity that sells your book, such as a bookstore or website. Alternatively, it can refer to someone who provides a service related to the creation of you book, such as an editor or printer.

widget (shopping cart/otherwise): A widget is a little button on your website that provides a link to something else. You probably see widgets everywhere without even noticing. Your website should have widgets that make it so people can easily share your content on social media as well as purchase your book.

ACKNOWLEDGMENTS

We know more than most how much work goes into bringing a book into the world. The people who help us, support us, and spread the word about our work, are the reason we get to write books like this. The community of collaborators we are privileged to call friends and fellow authors is special and we can't thank you enough. Though we are likely to forget a few folks (forgive us!) we want to thank the following people:

- The Wise Ink community of authors. You amazing folks are the best. You inspire, motivate, and empower us. You've become dear friends and your experiences have taught us more than could fit in this book. Thank you for trusting us on your journey.

- The Wise Ink Staff, specifically, Patrick and Graham of our production team. Thank you for reading this book two-hundred times, and helping us make it readable. Thank you also to our incredible interns who have played a part in getting this book into the hands of authors everywhere. Super special thanks and hugs to Amy Quale, Dara's business partner, work-spouse, and trusted friend.

- Athena Currier, our book designer, who over several months worked with us to implement every crazy design idea and make this book look spectacular.

- Our families, of course. Creative work is only possible with their support. Tomme & Genesis, you truly are Dara's favorites. Roseanne would like to give big, squishy hugs to LB, Anna B, and Mister B, forever and always.

ABOUT THE AUTHORS

Roseanne Cheng is a former high school English teacher and author of two young adult books, *The Take Back of Lincoln Junior High* and *Edge the Bare Garden,* which won the gold medal for young adult fiction at the Writer's Digest Self Published Book Awards and the Moonbeam Children's Book Awards. She now works as Marketing Director at Wise Ink Creative Publishing where she holds the secondary title of "Author Therapist" and has the pleasure of helping authors create plans to get their work into the world. When she's not reading a book or practicing yoga, you can probably find her hanging out with her hilarious husband of ten years and their two ridiculously awesome kids. Follow her on Twitter @teachablelit.

Dara Beevas believes that books can save lives, open doors, and build bridges. As co-founder of Wise Ink, she encourages authors to share powerful stories that ignite change, tolerance, and growth. She has been involved in the publishing community for fifteen years, acquiring manuscripts, managing projects, and creating marketing and sales strategies for authors and publishers. She's helped more than four hundred authors publish their books. She is the author of *The Indie Author Revolution* and co-author of *Social Media Secrets for Authors*. When she's not busy pushing the envelope in this crazy world of publishing and networking with inspiring entrepreneurs, she's traveling and enjoying her husband Tomme's delicious Jamaican meals with her daughter Genesis. Follow her on Twitter and Instagram at @darairene.

C

CONTACT WISE INK

To get the latest Wise Ink updates and resources, visit:

www.Wiseink.com

At Wise Ink, we frequently speak on the topics of writing, indie publishing, marketing, and platform building. We are happy to craft a keynote, half-day, or full-day version of this content for your classroom, writer's group, or business. If you're interested in exploring this possibility, email us at:

editor@wiseink.com

You can also connect with Wise Ink here:

Twitter: twitter.com/wiseink
Facebook: facebook.com/wiseinkpub
Instagram: instagram.com/wise_ink
Pinterest: pinterest.com/wiseink

And if you're working on a book and want to chat with us about helping you publish it, you can reach us at:

T: 612-605-1775
E: editor@wiseink.com

Made in the USA
Columbia, SC
11 July 2019